The Book of Assistance

Other Related Fons Vitae Titles

Three Early Sufi Texts:
A Treatise on the Heart
Bayan al-Farq bayn al-Sadr wa-al-Qalb wa-al-Fu'ad wa-al-Lubb
Attributed to Al-Hakim Al-Tirmidhi (D. C. 300/912)
Introduced and Translated by Nicholas Heer

Stations of the Righteous (*Darajat al-sadiqin*) &
The Stumblings of those Aspiring (*Zalal al-fuqara'*):
TwoTexts on the Path of Blame
by Abu 'abd Al-Rahman Al-Sulami Al-Naysaburi (D. 412/1021)
Introduced and Translated by Kenneth L.Honerkamp

Me and Rumi: The Autobiography of Shems-i Tabrizi
Translated, Introduced and Annotated by William C. Chittick

The Lives of Man–A Guide to the Human States:
Before Life, In the World, and After Death
by Imam 'Abd Allah ibn 'Alawi al-Haddad, Translated by Mostafa al-Badawi

The Degrees of the Soul
by Shaykh Abd Al-Khaliq Al-Shabrawi, Tranlated by Mostafa Al-Badawi

Early Sufi Women
by Abu Abd ar-Rahman as-Sulami, Translated by Rkia E. Cornell

The Autobiography of a Moroccan Soufi: Ahmad Ibn Ajiba
Translated by Jean-Louis Michon and from the French by David Streight

Al-Ghazali's Path to Sufism–his Deliverance from Error
al-Munqidh min al-Dalal
Translated by R.J. McCarthy with a Preface by David Burrell
and Introduction by William A. Graham

Al Ghazali Faith in Divine Unity & Trust in Divine Providence
Translated with an Introduction by David B. Burrell

Letters of Sufi Master: The Shaykh ad-Darqawi
Translated by Titus Burckhardt with a Foreword by Martin Lings

The Name & the Named
Compiled by Shaykh Tosun Bayrak al-Jerrahi al-Halveti
with a Foreword by William C. Chittick

Ibn Arabi Divine Governance of the Human Kingdom
Interpreted by Shaykh Tosun Bayrak al-Jerrahi al-Halveti

Suhrawardi The Shape of Light
Interpreted by Shaykh Tosun Bayrak al-Jerrahi al-Halveti

The Book of Assistance

By
Imam ‘Abd Allah ibn ‘Alawi al-Haddad

FONS VITAE

Second edition
This edition printed and distributed by
Fons Vitae, Louisville, Kentucky

Library of Congress Control Number: 2003113441

ISBN-1-887752-58-7

This edition published by
Fons Vitae
49 Mockingbird Valley Drive
Louisville, KY 40207-1366
fonsvitaeky@aol.com
www.fons vitae.com

Cover photo: © ARAMCO World, PADIA, Brynn Bruign

Cover design by *Folio*.

Printed in Canada

Contents

TRANSLATOR'S PREFACE

The Messenger of God, may blessings and peace be upon him and upon his family, prophesied that in every century God would raise up amongst his nation a man who would renew its religion. Imām 'Abd Allāh al-Ḥaddād was the renewer, or *Mujaddid*, of the twelfth Islamic century. He was renowned, and deservedly so, for the breadth of his knowledge and his manifest sanctity. The profundity of his influence on Muslims is reflected by the fact that his books are still in print throughout the Islamic world.

He was born in Tarīm, in the hills of Ḥaḍramaut, one of the southerly regions of the Arabian peninsula, and grew up in an environment where the accent was upon piety, frugality, erudition, and an uncompromising thirst for *ma'rifa* or direct contemplative knowledge. His lineage is traced back to the Prophet, may blessings and peace be upon him, and his family, through Imām al-Ḥusayn. His illustrious ancestors, the 'Alawī *sādāt*, had for centuries produced generation after generation of great scholars, gnostics, and summoners to the Straight Path.

Imām al-Ḥaddād's writings, if we except a few short treatises, and his volume of poetry, are mostly concerned with establishing within his readers the firmest possible foundations for faith and certainty. He recognized the signs of his times, and of the times to come, and observed how people were drawing away from religion, exhibiting a reluctance to study and a diminishing inclination to seek spiritual growth. He therefore endeavored to produce concise, clear, and uncontroversial texts. His concern for brevity is manifest throughout his books, many of which are abbreviated adaptations of Imām al-Ghazālī's monumental *Revival of the Religious Sciences* [*Iḥyā' 'Ulūm al-Dīn*]. Ghazālī had himself been the renewer of the sixth century.

Imām al-Ḥaddād died on the eve of the seventh of Dhū al-Qa'da, 1132 AH, having spent his life bringing people to their Lord through his oral and written teaching, and his exemplary life.

He was buried in a simple grave in the cemetery at Tarīm.

The present translation is one of the works which he designed as guides for Muslims who 'earnestly desire to tread the path of the Afterlife,' and seriously follow the *Sunna* of the Prophet, may blessings and peace be upon him and his family.

In the original there are neither chapter numbers, titles, nor annotations. We have therefore numerated and titled every chapter, appended a glossary, and added a few notes where this seemed appropriate. Quotations from the Qur'ān are based on Pickthall's translation, and are followed by *sūra* and verse numbers.

Whenever difficulties arose in understanding the text, or deciding between different possible interpretations, the help of *Sayyid* Aḥmad Mashhūr al-Ḥaddād was sought. Being the spiritual heir of Imām al-Ḥaddād, he is undoubtedly the best qualified person to comment on his writings. It is entirely through their *baraka* and assistance that the work was brought to completion; may God reward them on our behalf as befits the exaltation of their spiritual rank.

MOSTAFA AL-BADAWI

Al-Madina al-Munawwara,
Ramadan 1408

THE BOOK OF ASSISTANCE, SUPPORT AND ENCOURAGEMENT FOR SUCH BELIEVERS AS DESIRE TO FOLLOW THE WAY OF THE AFTERLIFE

In the Name of God, Most-Merciful and Compassionate. Lord, make it easy and give assistance, O Generous One! Grant us truth for You are the One who grants, the Knowing. ***Transcendent are You! We have no knowledge save that which You have taught us; You are indeed the Knowing, the Wise.***[1]

ALL PRAISE BELONGS TO GOD, the One, the Munificent, the Bestowing, the Provider, the Solicitous, the Benevolent, who sent Muḥammad, the Seal of His Prophets—may God's blessings and peace be upon him—with His Message to all men and jinn, revealed to him ***the Qur'ān in which is guidance for the people and clear indications for guidance and discernment,***[2] ordained for him and his community that which He had enjoined upon Noah, Abraham, Moses and Jesus,[3] gave supremacy to his religion over all others, made him the most honorable of all creation in His sight, and made his community the best community ever brought out for mankind, believing in God and the Last Day, enjoining good and forbidding evil,[4] assisting each other in benevolence and God-fearing (*taqwā*) and not helping each other in sin and aggression,[5] establishing the Ritual Prayer, paying out the *Zakāt*,[6]

---

1. Qur'ān, 2:32

2. ***The month of Ramaḍān in which the Qur'ān was revealed, a guidance for mankind and clear indications for guidance and discernment.*** Qur'ān, 2:185.

3. ***He has ordained for you that religion which He enjoined upon Noah, and that which We revealed to you, and that which We enjoined upon Abraham, Moses, and Jesus.*** Qur'ān, 42:13.

4. ***You are the best community that has ever been brought out for mankind: you enjoin good and forbid evil, and you believe in God.*** Qur'ān, 3:110

5. ***Help one another in benevolence and God-fearing, but help not one another in sin and aggression; indeed, God is severe in punishment.*** Qur'ān, 5:2.

6. *Zakāt* is the obligatory annual tax on wealth to be distributed to the poor as prescribed by the Qur'ān.

giving each other counsels of truth and fortitude,[7] and fighting in the way of God, fearless of the criticism of those who are devious and forsaken. For only those in whom have come true God's words of wretchedness, failure, disgrace, and humiliation, attempt to drive people away from God and denigrate those who give Him His due; and only those destined by God for happiness, safety, triumph, and felicity, devote themselves totally to counseling God's servants and inviting them to Him. These are the Prophet's heirs, the leaders of the God-fearing, and the best in the sight of the Lord of the Worlds, believers firmly grounded in knowledge, who experience the realities of faith, certainty and excellence, and attain through unveiling and contemplation to the secrets of God's visible and invisible domains. They only attain to these merits and achieve such ranks through the excellence of their following in the footsteps of the Leader of all Leaders, whom God has sent as a Mercy to the Worlds, who is God's slave, His Messenger, beloved and intimate friend, our master Muḥammad—may God's blessings and peace be upon him, his family, and Companions; and may these blessings be repeated each instant and perpetuated for as long as God, the Sovereign, the Judge, abides.

To proceed: the poor servant, confessing his shortcomings and limitations, hoping for the pardon of his Able Lord, the sharīf[8] 'Abd Allāh ibn 'Alawī al-Ḥaddād Bā-'Alawī al-Ḥusaynī—may God forgive him and his ancestors—says:

This is a treatise which is—by God's ability and power—comprehensive, containing counsels which will be—by God's grace and mercy—beneficial. I was moved to write it by the wish to obey the commands of God and of His Messenger, and the desire for the true promise made to those who give guiding directions, invite to goodness, and spread knowledge. God the Ex-

7. ***By the declining Day! Man is indeed in a state of loss, except those who believe and do good works, and exhort each other to truth and exhort each other to fortitude***. Qur'ān, 103:1, 2, 3.

8. A sharīf is a nobleman, in this context a descendent of the Prophet—may God's blessings and peace be upon him and his family. In the Ḥijāz they term sharīf those of the Prophet's descendents who in olden days were martially inclined, carried weapons, and to whom belonged the governorship of Makka, whereas they term sayyid those descendents of the Prophet who are scholars or students. Elsewhere the two terms are synonymous.

alted says, ***Let there be among you a community who invite to goodness, enjoin good, and forbid evil; those are the successful.***[9] And He says, Exalted is He, ***Summon to the way of your Lord with wisdom and fair exhortation.***[10] And He says, Exalted is He, ***And when God took the pledge of those who had been given the Book: You should make it clear to the people and not conceal it.***[11] And He said to His Prophet, ***Say, "This is my way; I summon to God clear-sightedly, I and those who follow me."***[12]

And the Messenger of God—may God's blessings and peace be upon him—said, *Let those who are present inform those who are absent,*[13] *for one may carry knowledge to another who is more knowledgeable than he, and one may carry knowledge who is not himself knowledgeable.*[14] And he said, may blessings and peace be upon him, *He who summons to guidance receives a reward equal to those who follow him, without this diminishing theirs in any way; and he who summons to error will have sinned as much as all those who follow him, without this diminishing their sins in any way.*[15] And he said, may blessings and peace be upon him and his family, *He who indicates goodness obtains as much reward as he who actually does it.*[16] And he said, may blessings and peace be upon him and his family, *When a man dies, his works come to an end except for three: an ongoing charity, knowledge of which use is made, and a righteous son who prays for him.*[17] And he said, may blessings and peace be upon him and his family, *The most generous among you after me will be a man who acquires knowledge and spreads it; he will be raised on Resurrection Day as a community unto himself.*[18] And he said, may blessings and peace be upon him and his family, *All creatures pray for the one who*

9. Qur'ān, 3:104.
10. Qur'ān, 21:125.
11. Qur'ān, 3:187.
12. Qur'ān, 12:108.
13. Nasā'ī, *al-Sunan al-Kubrā*, 4078; Ibn Ḥibbān, Ṣaḥīḥ, 5973; Aḥmad, *Musnad*, 20419.
14. Abū Dāwūd, *Sunan*, 3660; Tirmidhī, *Sunan*, 2656 -2658.
15. Muslim, Ṣaḥīḥ, 2674.
16. Muslim, Ṣaḥīḥ, 1893.
17. Muslim, Ṣaḥīḥ, 1631.
18. Bayhaqī, *Shu'ab al-Īmān,* 1632; Abū Ya'lā, *Musnad*, 2790.

teaches goodness, even the fish in the water.[19] And he said, may blessings and peace be upon him and his family, *All human beings are dependents of God, and the dearest to God are those who are of most benefit to His dependents.*[20]

None can be of more benefit to God's created beings than those who invite them to His door by teaching them what is due to Him in the way of *Tawḥīd* and obedience, reminding them of His signs and graces, giving them tidings of His Mercy, and also warnings of His wrath which strikes those who expose themselves to it, whether they are disbelievers or merely transgressors. I was prompted to obey this formidable command and was reinforced in my wish to attain to the generous promise made in the aforementioned verses and *ḥadīths*,[21] as well as others which I have not mentioned, by a truthfully aspiring brother, a sayyid who treads the path to felicity, who requested me to write to him with a counsel from which he would profit.[22] I have answered him through the aforementioned desire to obey God's commands, win His reward, and obtain His assistance, hoping that He—Exalted is He—will attend to my needs, as His Messenger—may God's blessings and peace be upon him—has said, *He who is engaged in fulfilling his brother's need, God fulfills his;*[23] and *God continues to assist His servant so long as the servant is assisting his brother.*[24]

I seek God's forgiveness and do not claim that my intention in writing this treatise is confined to these virtuous religious purposes; how can I when I am well aware of the hidden desires, egotistic passions, and worldly wishes that I harbor? ***I do not claim innocence for myself; the ego is indeed an inciter to evil, save when my Lord shows mercy; my Lord is indeed Forgiving, Com-***

19. Daylamī, *Musnad al-Firdaws,* 2996.

20. Bayhaqī, *Shu'ab al-Īmān,*7046- 7047; Abū Ya'lā, *Musnad*, 3315; Bazzār, *Musnad*, 6947.

21. A *ḥadīth* is a Prophetic utterance, a tradition authenticated by one or more chains of transmission and preserved in one or more of the extant compilations of *ḥadīth*.

22. This is Sayyid Aḥmad ibn Hāshim al-Ḥabashī, one of the Imām's childhood friends.

23. Bukhārī, *Ṣaḥīḥ*, 2442; Muslim, *Ṣaḥīḥ*, 2580.

24. Muslim, *Ṣaḥīḥ*, 2699.

passionate.[25] The ego is an enemy, and an enemy should never be trusted. It is in effect the worst of enemies; as the Messenger of God—may God's blessings and peace be upon him—has said, *Your worst enemy is your ego which is between your two flanks*.[26]

How inspired is the verse of the poet:

Beware of your ego, and trust not its mischief;
For the ego is worse than seventy devils.

O God, I seek your protection against my associating [*shirk*][27] knowingly, and Your forgiveness for that of which I am not aware!

I have begun each chapter in this treatise by saying, "You must do such-and-such a thing!" this being addressed first to my own self, then to my brother who was the cause for writing this treatise, and then generally to every Muslim who reads it. This expression has an effect on the heart of those it is addressed to, and I hope that, having used it, I will escape the reproaches and threats under which are those who say but do not do, and know but do not act. For when I address myself, saying, "You must do this!" this indicates that the thing has yet to become a reality when I do practice what I know, and that I am still at the stage of prompting myself to practice what I preach. In this manner, I will neither be deceiving the believers, nor forgetting myself, for this is how God describes those who have little understanding: ***Will you exhort people to goodness and forget yourselves, even as you recite the Book? Have you no understanding?***[28] I will thus be saved from the threats directed at those who speak but do not act, as in the words of the Messenger of God—may God's blessings and peace be upon him and his family: *A man will be brought on Resurrection Day and cast into the Fire where his entrails will spill out, and there he will turn just like a donkey in a mill. The people in the Fire will gather around him and say, "What is with you; did you not enjoin good upon us and forbid evil?" He will reply, "I*

25. Qur'ān, 12:53.

26. Bayhaqī, *Kitāb al-Zuhd al-Kabīr,* 343; Abū 'Abd al-Raḥmān al-Sulamī, *Ādāb al-Suḥba,* 68.

27. *Shirk*: Association of other deities with God. It is rendered as either polytheism or idolatry according to the context.

28. Qur'ān, 2:44.

enjoined good but did not do it and forbade evil but committed it."[29] And, *The scholar who teaches others but does not practice what he knows is as the wick that gives light to others while burning itself.*[30] And, *When I was made to journey by night I passed by men whose lips were being clipped with scissors of fire. I asked Gabriel, "Who are these?" and he replied, "Worldly preachers who enjoined good, but neglected to do it, even as they recited the Book. Could they not understand?"*[31]

These threats come true for those who summon to God but whose real intention is to acquire the things of this world; who exhort to good, yet persistently abandon it; who warn against evil, yet persistently commit it; and who fall into ostentation, wishing to make a reputation for themselves. As for those who summon others to God's door while upbraiding their own egos, forbidding them to be neglectful, and exhorting them to show zeal, it is to be hoped that they will be saved. Anyway, he who knows and teaches, but does not practice what he knows, is in a better state, a wiser way, and has a safer outcome than he who knows but neither practices nor teaches.

A man of little understanding may perhaps say, "There is already a sufficient abundance of books; there is no benefit in compiling new ones at this stage." Such a man is correct insofar as books are indeed abundant and should be sufficient, but not in saying that no benefit is to be gained from compiling new ones. People's hearts are naturally attracted to everything new, and God gives them, with each moment, knowledge clothed in the form best suited to their times. Books reach distant places and survive the scholar's death; he thus stands to receive the merit of spreading knowledge and to be counted by God among the teachers and summoners to Him, even after he has entered his grave. As the Messenger of God—may God's blessings and peace be upon him—has said, *He whose speech revives a truth that those after*

---

29. Muslim, *Ṣaḥīḥ*, 2989.

30. This a paraphrase of a *ḥadīth* that says, *The likeness of he who teaches the people good things but forgets himself is that of a wick that gives light to others while burning itself.* [Ṭabarānī, *Kabīr*, 1681; Daylamī, *Musnad al-Firdaws*, 6419.]

31. Bayhaqī, *Shu'ab al-Īmān*, 4614; Aḥmad, *Musnad*, 12211; Bazzār, *Musnad*, 7418.

him practice continues to receive its reward until Resurrection Day...[32]

I have called the treatise *The Book of Assistance, Support, and Encouragement for Such Believers as Desire to Follow the Way of the Afterlife.*

I ask God to make me and other believers benefit from it and to render my compilation of it purely for the sake of His Noble Countenance.

It is now time to begin. Success is from God; I seek His help, depend on Him entirely, and ask Him to grant me success in being correct in my intentions, words, and deeds. He is worthy of this and Able to grant it. He is my sufficiency and the Best of Patrons.

32. Aḥmad, *Musnad*, 13803; Bayhaqī, *Shu'ab al-Īmān,* 7276.

Chapter 1

On Certainty

You must, beloved brother, strengthen and improve your certainty. For when certainty prevails in the heart and is firmly established therein, the unseen becomes as if seen, and the man of certainty says, as 'Alī—may God honor his face—once said, "Were the cover to be removed, I would not increase in certainty."

Certainty is power, firmness, and stability of faith so great that it becomes a towering mountain which no doubt can shake and no illusion rock. Rather, doubts and illusions disappear completely, and whenever they come from the exterior are neither listened to by the ear nor heeded by the heart. The Devil cannot approach the possessor of such certainty; on the contrary, he flees from him, fears his very shadow, and is content to keep at a safe distance. As the Messenger of God—may God's blessings and peace be upon him—said, *The Devil is afraid of you 'Umar.*[1] *Never does 'Umar take a road but that the Devil takes another.*[2]

Certainty becomes more powerful and excellent through various means. The first, most essential and pivotal of these is that the servant listen attentively with his heart as well as his ears to the verses and *ḥadīths* relating to the Majesty of God—Exalted is He, His is perfection, magnitude, and grandeur, He being the sole creator and decision maker, the sole irresistible sovereign—and likewise listen to the truthfulness and perfection of the Divine Envoys, the miracles they were confirmed with, the sundry chastisements which befell those who opposed them, and know that there will be reward in the hereafter for those who behave well and chastisement for those who do evil. That these are sufficient to bring about certainty is indicated by His words, Exalted is He, ***Is it not sufficient for them that We sent down upon you the Book which is recited to them?***[3]

1. Tirmidhī, *Sunan*, 3690.
2. Bukhārī, *Ṣaḥīḥ*, 3683; Muslim, *Ṣaḥīḥ*, 2396.
3. Qur'ān, 29:51.

The second is to learn from observing the kingdom of the heaven and the earth, and the wondrous and astounding creatures that God made them teem with. That this brings about certainty is indicated by His saying, Exalted is He, ***We shall show them our signs on the horizons and within themselves until it becomes clear to them that it is the truth***.[4]

The third is to behave, both outwardly and inwardly, according to what one believes, zealously, and to the limits of one's resources. That this brings about certainty is indicated by his saying, Exalted is He, ***Those who strive in Us We shall most surely guide to our ways***.[5]

Among the results of certainty are serene belief in God's promise, confidence in what He has guaranteed, attending to God with all of one's being, abandoning all things which distract from Him, continuously returning to Him in all circumstances, and spending one's entire energy in seeking His good pleasure.

In sum, certainty is the essential thing, while all other noble ranks, praiseworthy traits of character, and good works, are its branches and results.

Virtues and actions are strong or weak, sound or unsound, according to the strength of certainty. Luqmān—may peace be upon him—said, "Action is possible only in the presence of certainty; a servant acts in obedience only to the extent that he has certainty and becomes neglectful only when his certainty diminishes." This is why the Messenger of God—may God's blessings and peace be upon him—has said, *Certainty is the whole of faith*.[6]

Believers possess three degrees of certainty. The first is that of the People of the Right Hand,[7] which is firm belief, but with

---

4. Qur'ān, 41:53.

5. Qur'ān, 29:69.

6. Al-Shihāb, *Musnad*, 158; Bayhaqī, *Shu'ab al-Īmān*, 9265; Abū Nu'aym, *Ḥilyat al-Awliyā'*, 5:34. The *ḥadīth* in its entirety says, *Patience is half of faith and certainty the whole of faith*.

7. In *Sūra al-Wāqi'a* (The Event) [Qur'ān, 56] people are classified into three kinds: those on the right-hand side, those on the left-hand side, and the Foremost, who are the Ones Brought Near. The People of the Right Hand are the multitude of common believers who will enter the Garden and be spared the Fire. They are said to be, ***A multitude of those of old and a multitude of those of later time***. [Qur'ān, 56:39, 40]. The People of the Left Hand are those who will

the possibility of becoming doubtful or shaky under certain circumstances. This is called faith.

The second is that of the Ones Brought Near, which is when the heart is filled with faith so firmly established therein that its opposite becomes no longer possible or even conceivable. In this degree the unseen becomes as the seen. This is called certainty.

The third is that of the Prophets and the Veracious [*Ṣiddīqūn*][8] who are their perfect heirs. Here the unseen becomes seen, which thing is called unveiling [*kashf*][9] and vision [*'ayān*].[10]

There are grades within each degree, all are good, but some better than others. ***That is God's grace, He bestows it upon whom He will; and God's grace is immense.***[11]

---

enter the Fire. Finally, the Foremost are those far ahead on the spiritual path who attain to direct knowledge and are said to be, ***A multitude of those of old and a few of those of later time.*** [Qur'ān, 56:13, 14]

8. The supreme saints, the Veracious, (*Ṣiddīqūn*) are the highest ranking among saints whose rank is immediately beneath that of the Prophets. They are the utterly sincere who, having withheld nothing from God, are withheld nothing of His grace.

9. *Kashf* is unveiling, which is the direct vision of the normally unseen subtle dimensions of existence.

10. *'Ayān* or vision is equivalent to *mushāhada* or contemplation, which is the direct perception of Divine realities.

11. Qur'ān, 57:29.

Chapter 2

On Intention

You must, my brother, improve the soundness and sincerity of your intentions, examine them, and reflect upon them well before embarking on your actions. For intentions are the bases of deeds; according to them your deeds will either be good or ugly, sound or unsound. The Prophet has said, may God's blessings and peace be upon him and his family, *Deeds are according to intentions; each man receives that which he had intended...*[1]

Therefore, you must utter no word, do no action, and decide no matter without the intention of drawing nearer thereby to God and seeking the reward He has assigned, through His beneficence and grace, to the intended act. Also know that drawing nearer to Him can only be done through the obligatory and supererogatory devotions that He has indicated through his Messenger—may God's blessings and peace be upon him and his family.

A sincere intention may turn the merely licit into the devotional, for means are judged according to their ends. For example, when one eats to acquire the strength to perform devotions, or sleeps with his wife to have a son who would worship God.

It is a condition of the sincere intention that behavior does not belie it. For instance, a man who seeks knowledge, claiming that his intention is to practice and teach it, will be proved insincere in his intention if, when he becomes able to, he fails to do so. Or a man who chases worldly goods, claiming that he is doing so only that he may be independent of others, be able to give charity to the needy, and help his relatives; he will be proved ineffectual in his intention should he fail to do so when able.

Intentions do not affect sins, just as purification does not affect that which is, by its very nature, impure. A man who goes along with another who is slandering a Muslim, then pretends that he only wanted to humor him, is himself a slanderer. He who re-

1. Bukhārī, *Ṣaḥīḥ*, 1; Muslim, *Ṣaḥīḥ*, 1907.

frains from enjoining good and forbidding evil, and then pretends that he only did so not to offend the culprit, is but his partner in evildoing. A malicious intention attached to a good deed spoils it and renders it malicious, as for example when one performs good deeds for the sake of wealth and prestige.

Always strive, my brother, to intend that your obedience be solely for the sake of God, and that whatever lawful things you may use are only to help you to obey Him.

Know that several intentions can attach to a single act and that each of them will attract its full reward. An example of this in devotional activities is when someone reads the Qur'ān intending to commune with God, which he will indeed be doing, but also to extract from it different kinds of knowledge, seeing that the Qur'ān is the very mine of knowledge, to profit those whose listen or [just happen to] hear, or any other good intention. And an example in permissible activities is to eat with the intention of obeying your Lord in His saying, Exalted is He, ***O believers, eat of the good things with which We have provided you and give thanks to God.***[2] Intend by so doing to acquire strength for devotion and to place yourself in a situation where you must thank your Lord, for He says - Transcendent is He, ***Eat of your Lord's provision and thank Him.***[3] These two examples can be applied analogously to all other devotional or merely permissible activities. Always do your best to increase your good intentions.

The word 'intention' can have one of two meanings. The first is the aim which makes you decide, do, or say something. Taken in this sense the intention is usually better than the act when the act is good and worse when the act is evil. He has said, may blessings and peace be upon him and his family, *The intention of a believer is better than his deed.*[4] Notice how he specifically mentions the believer. The second is when you decide and resolve to initiate the act. Taken in this sense it is not better than the act. A person who resolves to do something can only be in one of three situations.

[1] He decides and acts.

2. Qur'ān, 2: 172.
3. Qur'ān, 34:15.
4. Ṭabarānī, *Kabīr*, 5942.

[2] He decides but fails to act while able to.

The way to evaluate these two situations can be clearly found in that which Ibn 'Abbās[5]—may God be pleased with him and his father—has transmitted to the effect that the Messenger of God—may God's blessings and peace be upon him and his family—said, *God has written* [i.e. defined] *good and evil deeds, then rendered them clear; anyone who intends a good deed but does not perform it, God records it as one good deed, whereas should he intend and then perform it, God records it as ten good deeds, up to seven hundred fold, and to yet more multiplications. If he intends an evil deed and does not do it, God records it as one full good deed; if he intends and then does it, God records it as one evil deed.*[6]

[3] He decides upon something which he is for the time being unable to do and says, "Were I able, I would do [such-and-such a thing]." He receives the same as the one who acts, whether this is for or against him.

The evidence for this is his saying, may blessings and peace be upon him and his family, *The likeness of this community is that of four persons: a man to whom God has given knowledge and wealth: he uses his wealth according to his knowledge and spends it where it should; another to whom God has given knowledge but no wealth: he says, "Were God to give me as He has given him, I would do as he does." Their rewards are equal. And a man to whom God has given wealth but no knowledge, who mishandles his wealth and spends it where it should not; while another who was given neither knowledge nor wealth watches him and says, "Were I to have as He has, I would do as he does." Their burdens of sin are equal.*[7]

---

5. 'Abd Allāh ibn 'Abbās was the son of the Prophet's uncle al-'Abbās, and one of the seven Companions who have transmitted over one thousand *ḥadīths* each.

6. Bukhārī, *Ṣaḥīḥ*, 6491; Muslim, *Ṣaḥīḥ*, 207.

7. Ibn Māja, *Sunan*, 4228.

Chapter 3

On Vigilance

You must my brother be mindful of God the Exalted in all your movements and halts, at every moment, with every blink of the eye, with every thought, wish, or any other state. Feel His nearness to you! Know that He looks and is aware of you, and that nothing that you conceal is hidden from Him, ***nothing that weighs so much as an atom is hidden from your Lord, whether on earth or in heaven.***[1] ***When you speak aloud He knows your secret [thought] and that which is even more hidden.***[2] He is with you wherever you are with His knowledge, awareness and power. If you are righteous, He will guide, assist and protect you.

Therefore, be modest before your Lord as you should; make sure He never sees you in a situation which He has forbidden you, or misses you where He has commanded you to be; worship Him as if you saw Him, for even if you do not see Him, He sees you. Whenever you notice in your soul any laziness in His worship or inclination for disobedience, remind it that God hears and sees you and knows what you secretly whisper to yourself or to others. If this reminding does not benefit it because of the inadequacy of its knowledge of the Majesty of God, remind it of the two noble angels who record good and evil deeds, and recite to it, ***When the two receivers***[3] ***receive, sitting on the right and on the left, he utters no word but there is with him a watcher, ready.***[4] If this reminding does not influence it, remind it of the proximity of death, that it is the nearest of all hidden and awaited things; frighten it of its sudden pouncing, whereby if it does come when it is in an unsatisfactory state, it will end up in endless perdition.

---

1. Qur'ān, 10:61.
2. Qur'ān, 20:7.
3. The two receivers are the angels who record a person's deeds: the right angel for good and the left for evil deeds.
4. Qur'ān, 50:17, 18.

If this threat is of no use, remind it of the immense reward that God promises those who obey Him and the painful torment with which He threatens those who disobey Him. Say to it, "O Soul, after death there will be no opportunity to repent, and there is nothing, after this life, other than the Garden or the Fire. Choose if you will obedience, the consequence of which is triumph, contentment, immortality in vast gardens, and gazing at the Face of God, the Generous, the Beneficent; or disobedience, the consequence of which is degradation, humiliation, mockery, deprivation, and imprisonment between layers of fire." Endeavor to cure your soul with such reminders when it neglects obedience and inclines to rebellion, for they are useful medicines for the heart's diseases.

If you find, emerging in your heart when you call to mind the fact that God observes you, a shyness that prevents you from disobeying Him and drives you to exert yourself in obeying Him, then you are in possession of something of the realities of vigilance [*murāqaba*]

Know that vigilance is one of the most noble stations, high positions, and lofty degrees. It is the Station of Excellence [*iḥsān*] indicated in the Prophet's saying, may God's blessings and peace be upon him and his family, *Excellence is to worship God as if you see him, for if you see Him not, He sees you.*[5] All the faithful believe that nothing on earth or in heaven is concealed from God, that God is with them wherever they are, and that none of their movements or standstills are concealed from Him. But the important thing is that this awareness be permanent and that its results appear, the least of which is that the person does nothing, when alone with God, that he would be ashamed of should a man of virtue see him. This is rare, and it eventually leads to that which is rarer still, whereby the servant is totally immersed in God the Exalted, extinct in Him and thus unaware of all else, absent from creation through contemplating the True King, having arrived at ***a secure seat in the presence of an Able Sovereign***.[6]

5. Bukhārī, *Ṣaḥīḥ*, 4777; Muslim, *Ṣaḥīḥ*, 1.
6. Qur'ān, 54:55.

Chapter 4

On the Inner and Outer Self

You must, my brother, improve your inward until it becomes better than your virtuous outward appearance, for the former is where the gaze of the Real obtains, whereas the latter is subject to the gaze of created beings. God the Exalted never mentions the inward and the outward in His Book without beginning with the inward. And the Prophet used to pray, may peace be upon him, *O God, make my inward better than my outward, and make my outward virtuous.*[1]

When the inward is virtuous, the outward is also inevitably so, for the outward always follows the inward, whether for good or evil. The Messenger of God—may God's blessings and peace be upon him and his family—has said, *In the body is a small piece of flesh; when it is good the rest of the body is good, but when it is corrupt the rest of the body becomes corrupt: this is the heart.*[2]

Know that he who claims to have a thriving inward but whose outward is corrupted by his abandoning outward acts of obedience is but a pretender and a liar.

He who exerts himself to reform his outward by caring about the way he dresses, looks, speaks, moves, sits, stands, or walks, but leaves his inward full of repellent attributes and vile traits, is but one afflicted with affectation and ostentation, who has turned away from the Lord.

Beware, O brother, of doing in secret that which if seen by people would make you ashamed and worried about being censured. A Knower[3] once said, "A Sufi is not a Sufi unless, were everything within him to be exposed to everyone on a plate in

1. Tirmidhī, *Sunan*, 3586.

2. Bukhārī, *Ṣaḥīḥ*, 52; Muslim, *Ṣaḥīḥ*, 1599.

3. A Knower by God is a saint who has reached such a stage in soul purification that he sees, hears, walks, and does things by God's power, not his own, so that he can see, hear, and do what others cannot.

the marketplace, he would be ashamed of nothing that comes to light."

If you cannot make your inward better than your outward, the least that you can do is to make them equal, so that you behave equally well in private and in public in obeying God's injunctions, avoiding His prohibitions, respecting what He has made sacred, and hastening to please Him. This is the first step a servant takes on the path of special knowledge. Know this! Success is from God.

Chapter 5

On Regular Devotions

You must occupy your time with acts of worship so that no period elapses, whether at night or by day, without being used in some act of goodness. This is how the *baraka* within time is brought out, the purpose of life fulfilled, and concentration on God the Exalted sustained.

You should allocate specific periods of time for your habitual activities such as eating, drinking, and working for a livelihood.

Know that no state can be sound in the presence of neglect, nor can consequences be good in the presence of heedlessness.

The Proof of Islam[1]—may God spread his benefit—says, "You should structure your time, arrange your regular devotions [*awrād*] and assign to each function a set period of time during which it is given first priority but which it does not overstep. For if you abandon yourself to neglect and purposelessness, as cattle do, and just do anything that may occur to you at any time it happens to occur to you, most of your time will be wasted. Your time is your life, and your life is your capital; it is the basis of your commerce [with God], and the means to attain to everlasting felicity, in the proximity of God the Exalted. Each of your breaths is a priceless (because irreplaceable) jewel, and once it passes away it never returns."

You should not occupy all your time with only one *wird*,[2] even if it be the best, for you would then miss the *baraka* of multiplying and varying your *awrād*. Each *wird* has a particular ef-

---

1. The Proof of Islam (*Ḥujjat al-Islām*) is Imām Abū Ḥāmid al-Ghazālī. Born in Ṭūs in Khurāsān in 450 A.H, he wrote about two hundred books and treatises, the most important and best known of which is *Iḥyā' 'Ulūm al-Dīn* [*Revival of the Religious Sciences*]. He died in 505 A.H.

2. A *wird*, plural *awrād*, is any regularly repeated devotional act.

fect on the heart, a light, a flow of assistance [*madad*],[3] and a rank with God that it shares with no other. Furthermore, when you move from one *wird* to another you escape becoming bored, indolent, impatient, or weary. Ibn 'Aṭā'illāh al-Shādhilī—may God have mercy on him—says, "Aware of the boredom you may be subject to, the Real made acts of obedience varied."

Know that *awrād* have a great effect in illuminating the heart and controlling the senses, but these only appear and become established with perseverance, repetition, and performance at specifically allocated times.

If you are not one of those who occupy their night and daytime hours with devotional activities, then assign to yourself some *awrād* to persevere with at specific times, and make up for them if you ever miss them, so that your soul becomes accustomed to keeping to them. Once your soul despairs of your abandoning them altogether when you miss them, it will hasten to perform them in time. My master, Shaykh 'Abd al-Raḥmān al-Saqqāf—may God be pleased with him—has said, "He who has no *wird* is a *qird* [monkey]!" Another Knower said, "The arrival of the *wārid*[4] depends on the *wird*; therefore, he who outwardly has no *wird* will receive no inward *wārid*."

Be moderate and keep to the middle way in everything. Choose those acts which you are capable of persevering in. The Messenger of God—may God's blessings and peace be upon him and his family—has said, *The acts most pleasing to God are the most constant, even if few.*[5] And he has said, may peace be upon him, *Choose the acts of which you are capable, for God never grows weary before you do.*[6]

It is the Devil's way to entice the disciple [*murīd*] at the beginning of his quest to multiply to excess his devotional activities, the purpose being to cause him eventually to retreat, either by giving up acts of goodness altogether, or performing them incor-

---

3. *Madad* means assistance, support, and reinforcement, whether material or spiritual.

4. The *wārid*, plural *wāridāt*, means something that arrives. In this context this will be gifts of light, serenity, inspiration, or direct knowledge of God.

5. Bukhārī, *Ṣaḥīḥ*, 6464; Muslim, *Ṣaḥīḥ*, 783.

6. Bukhārī, *Ṣaḥīḥ*, 1970; Muslim, *Ṣaḥīḥ*, 782.

rectly, and the Accursed cares little with which of these two he afflicts him.

Awrād usually take the form of supererogatory prayers, Qur'ān recitations, the acquisition of knowledge, invocation [*dhikr*],[7] or reflection [*fikr*].

We shall now mention some of the proprieties with which these religious activities need to be performed.

You must have a *wird* of supererogatory prayers, in addition to the textually established ones, and should assign a definite time for it and a definite number which you can constantly sustain. Some of our virtuous predecessors—may God have mercy on them—had a *wird* of one thousand *rak'as* each day and night. Such, for instance, was 'Alī son of al-Ḥusayn—may God be pleased with them both; others had a *wird* of five hundred, three hundred, and so on.

Know that the Ritual Prayer has an outward form and an inward reality. Unless both are done properly, it will be considered worthless by God. As for its outward form, it consists of its formal obligations and proprieties such as correct standing, recitation, bowing, prostration, *tasbīḥ*, and so forth. As for its reality, it is that one be present with God, sincerely intend it to be purely for His sake, approach Him with complete resolution, collect one's heart so that one's thoughts are restricted to the Prayer and nothing else, and maintain the courtesies necessary for communing with God. He has said, may blessings and peace be upon him and his family, *He who is praying is communing with his Lord.*[8] And he has said, may blessings and peace be upon him and his family, *When the servant rises to his Prayer, God turns His Face toward him.*[9]

You should not occupy yourself with unspecified supererogatory prayers at a time designated for a *Sunna* which the Messenger of God either did or spoke about until you have completed the maximum designated number. An example of this is the *rak'as*

7. *Dhikr* means remembrance, invocation, making mention, and by extension a spiritual gathering. *Al-Dhikr*, "The Remembrance" is also one of the names of the Qur'ān.

8. Bayhaqī, *al-Sunan al-Kubrā*, 4704; Aḥmad, *Musnad*, 12063.

9. Ibn Māja, *Sunan*, 1023; Bazzār, *Sunan*, 2889.

laid down before and after the obligatory prayers. These are sufficiently well-known as to need no further comment. Another example is the *Witr* Prayer[10] which is a well established and certain prayer. Some scholars are of the opinion that it is obligatory. And the Messenger of God has said, may God's blessings and peace be upon him and his family, *God is* Witr *and He likes what is* witr; *therefore observe the* Witr, *O people of the Qur'ān.*[11] And, Witr *is truth. He is not of us who does not pray the* Witr.[12] Its maximum is eleven *rak'as* and its appropriate minimum three. For those who are well accustomed to get up for prayer during the latter part of the night it is better to leave it until then. He has said, may blessings and peace be upon him and his family, *Make your last night prayer the* Witr.[13] But those who have no such habit would do better to perform it after the *'Ishā'* prayer. A further example is the *Ḍuḥā* or Mid-Morning Prayer which is a very useful and blessed prayer. Its maximum is eight *rak'as*, though some have said twelve, and its minimum two. The best time for it is when the sun is high and about a quarter of the day has gone by. The Messenger of God—may God's blessings and peace be upon him—said, *Morning comes and on each of your phalanges a charity is due. Each* tasbīḥa [*glorification*] *is a charity, each* taḥmīda [*praise*] *a charity, each* tahlīla [*unification of God*] *a charity, each* takbīra [*magnification*] *a charity, and enjoining good and forbidding evil is charity. Two* rak'as *prayed in mid-morning will supply for all that.*[14] If this *Ṣaḥīḥ ḥadīth* had been the only one transmitted concerning the merit of this prayer it would have been sufficient. Yet another example is the prayer between *Maghrib* and *'Ishā'*. Its maximum is twenty *rak'as* and its average six. The Messenger of God—may God's blessings and peace be upon him—has said, *God erects a palace in the Garden for he who prays twenty* rak'as *between* Maghrib *and* 'Ishā'.[15] And he has said, may blessings and peace be upon him and his family, *He who prays six* rak'as *after*

10. *Witr* means odd as opposed to even. The 3, 5, 7, 9, or 11 *rak'as* to be performed at night are called *witr*.

11. Tirmidhī, *Sunan*, 453; Ibn Māja, *Sunan*, 1170.

12. Abū Dāwūd, *Sunan*, 1419; Aḥmad, *Musnad*, 23019.

13. Bukhārī, *Ṣaḥīḥ*, 998; Muslim, *Ṣaḥīḥ*, 751.

14. Muslim, *Ṣaḥīḥ*, 720; Abū Dāwūd, *Sunan*, 1286.

15. Ibn Māja, *Sunan*, 1373; Tirmidhī, *Sunan*, 435.

Maghrib *and does not speak ill between them will have them equal the worship of twelve years.*[16]

It is a *Sunna* to bring to life with devotions the period between the two Night Prayers. Many *ḥadīths* and other traditions have been transmitted regarding its merit. It should be enough to know that when Aḥmad ibn Abū al-Hawārī asked his Shaykh, Abū Sulaymān—may God have mercy on them—whether he should fast by day or bring to life the period between the two Night Prayers, he advised him to do both, to which he said, "I cannot, for if I fast I become occupied with breaking my fast at that time." He replied, "If you cannot do both, then leave daytime fasting and bring life to the time between the two Night Prayers." 'Ā'isha—may God be pleased with her—said, "The Messenger of God—may blessings and peace be upon him—never entered my house after the late night prayer [*'Ishā'*] without praying four or six *rak'as*."[17] And he said, may peace be upon him, *Four* rak'as *after* 'Ishā' *equal the same on* Laylat'ul-Qadr [*the Night of Destiny*].[18]

Pray at night, for he has said, may blessings and peace be upon him and his family, *The best prayer next to the prescribed ones is the night time prayer.*[19] And he has said, may blessings and peace be upon him and his family, *The superiority of nighttime over daytime is like the superiority of concealed over public charity.*[20] And it has been related that concealed charity is seventy times better then public charity.[21] He has said, may peace be upon him, *Keep rising at night to pray, for it was the way of the virtuous before you, it draws you nearer to your Lord, atones for your sins, forbids you from evil, and drives sickness away from the body.*[22] Know that the one who prays after *'Ishā'* is considered to have risen at night. Some of our predecessors used to pray their *wird* early in the night; however, rising after some sleep is a defeat

16. Ṭabarānī, *Awsaṭ*, 819; Tirmidhī, *Sunan*, 435; Ibn Māja, *Sunan*, 1167.
17. Nasā'ī, *al-Sunan al-Kubrā*, 390: Aḥmad, *Musnad*, 24305.
18. Ṭabarānī, *Awsaṭ*, 2733, 6332; Bayhaqī, *al-Sunan al-Kubrā*, 4188.
19. Muslim, *Ṣaḥīḥ*, 1163; Tirmidhī, *Sunan*, 438.
20. Bayhaqī, *Shu'ab al-Īmān,* 2832; Ṭabarānī, *Kabīr*, 10382.
21. Bayhaqī, *Shu'ab al-Īmān,*551, 552, 6394, 6451.
22. This version is in Ṭabarānī, *Kabīr*, 6154; There are other slightly different versions as in Tirmidhī, *Sunan*, 435.

for the Devil, an opposition to the ego, and contains a wondrous secret. This is the *tahajjud*[23] which God commanded His Messenger to do in his saying, ***Perform* tahajjud *by night, as an act of supererogation for you.***[24] It has been related that God wonders at a servant who rises from his bed, from his wife's side, to pray. He takes pride in him before his angels and turns His noble Face towards him. Know that it is reprehensible for the seeker of the hereafter not to rise at night; how [can he not] when a disciple should always be asking for more and exposing himself to His gifts at all times. For he has said, may blessings and peace be upon him and his family, *There is a time at night when no Muslim servant of God asks God for any of the good of this world or the next but that he is granted it. This happens every night.*[25]

In one of God's revealed scriptures it is said, "He has lied who claims to love Me but who, when night falls, sleeps and leaves Me. Does not every lover love to be alone with his beloved?"

Shaykh Ismā'īl ibn Ibrāhīm al-Jabartī—may God have mercy on him—has said, "God has gathered every goodness into the night, and no sainthood was ever formally granted to a saint except by night." My master al-'Aydarūs, 'Abd Allāh ibn Abū Bakr 'Alawī, has said, "He who wishes for the Lordly Purity should break himself in the depths of the night." The Messenger of God—may blessings and peace be upon him—has said, *God descends every night to the Terrestrial Heaven when only the last third of the night remains and says, "Is anyone praying, that I may answer him? Is anyone seeking forgiveness that I may forgive him? Is anyone requesting anything that I may grant him?" until the break of day.*[26] Had this been the only *ḥadīth* exhorting to night vigils it would have sufficed, so how must it be when both the Book and the *Sunna* are full of encouragements and exhortations to it? Knowers have in their night vigils noble unveilings and subtle experiences which they receive in their hearts, of the felicity of nearness to

---

23. Supererogatory night prayers in general are called *Qiyām*; but when one rises to pray after having slept a while are called *Tahajjud.*

24. Qur'ān, 17:19.

25. Muslim, *Ṣaḥīḥ*, 757.

26. Ṭabarānī, *al-Du'ā'*, 140. Slightly different versions are found in Bukhārī, *Ṣaḥīḥ*, 1145; Muslim, *Ṣaḥīḥ*, 758.

God, the pleasures of intimacy with Him and of communing and conversing with Him, Exalted is He. One of them has said, "If the state of the people of the Garden is similar to ours, they are indeed living pleasurably!" Another said, "The people of the night take more pleasure in their nights than the people of pleasures in their pleasures." And another said, "Nothing aggrieved me more during the last forty years than the break of dawn." However, this felicity occurs only after they have endured the bitterness and hardships that are in vigils. As 'Utba al-Ghulām said, "I endured the night for twenty years, then enjoyed it for twenty more."

Should you ask, "What should I recite during the night prayers, and how many *rak'as* should I pray?" then know that the Messenger of God—may blessings and peace be upon him—had no set recitation in his *tahajjud*. It is good to recite the Qur'ān, one part after another, so that you complete it in a month, or perhaps less or more according to your energy. As for the number of *rak'as*, the maximum that has been related of the Messenger of God—may blessings and peace be upon him—is thirteen; seven and nine have also been reported, but the most frequently reported figure is eleven.

The total purport of all the relevant *ḥadīths* is that it is recommended and encouraged, when you wake up, for you to rub sleep off your face with your hands and say, "Praised and thanked be God, who gave us life after causing us to die, and unto whom is the resurrection." Recite the last verses of *Sūra Āl-'Imrān* (The Family of 'Imrān),[27] then brush your teeth with the *siwāk*,[28] perform thorough *wuḍū'* [ritual ablution], pray two short *rak'as*, then add to them eight long ones. You can pray them in units of two, or four, or even do the full eight with only one salutation [*salām*], for all these have been reported. If you then find that you still have energy, pray any additional prayers that you may wish, then pray three *rak'as* as *Witr*, either with one salutation or two. Recite in the first *rak'a Sūra al-A'lā* (The Most High),[29] in the second *al-Kāfirūn* (The Disbelievers),[30] and in the third *al-Ikhlāṣ*

27. Qur'ān, 3: 190-200.
28. The *Siwāk* is a toothstick made from Arak tree branches.
29. Qur'ān, 87.
30. Qur'ān, 109.

(Sincerity),[31] and the last two *sūras*.[32]

Do not think that the *Witr* which is eleven *rak'as* is one thing and the *rak'as* we have just mentioned another. Only that which we have mentioned has been reported of the Messenger of God's night prayers. Know this! God is Vast and Knowing!

---

31. Qur'ān, 112.
32. Qur'ān, 113 and 114.

Chapter 6

On Reciting the Qur'ān

You must have a *wird* of reading or recitation[1] of the Mighty Book to be done every day. The minimum is to read one *juz'* [one thirtieth of the Qur'ān] so that you complete it once a month, and the maximum to complete it once every three days.

Know that immense merit attaches to reciting the Qur'ān and that it has a great influence in illuminating the heart. The Messenger of God—may blessings and peace be upon him—has said, *The best of my community's devotions is the recitation of the Qur'ān.*[2] And 'Alī—may God honor his face—has said, "He who recites the Qur'ān while standing in Prayer receives for each letter one hundred rewards; he who recites it sitting down in prayer receives for each letter fifty rewards; he who recites it outside the Prayer, but in a state of ritual purity, receives for each letter twenty-five rewards; and he who recites it without ritual purity receives for each letter ten rewards."

Beware of concentrating, while reciting, on the amount recited to the detriment of reflection and correct articulation. You must reflect and comprehend while you recite; slow, melodious recitation will assist you in this. Feel in your heart the magnitude of the Speaker—Transcendent and Exalted is He—and that you are before Him, reciting His Book to Him, in which He addresses His commands, prohibitions, counsels and exhortations to you. When reading verses of unification and glorification, be full of reverence and awe; when reading verses of promises and threats, be full of hopeful expectations mixed with apprehension; and when reading the commands and prohibitions, be thankful, acknowledge your shortcomings, ask for forgiveness, and resolve to show ardor.

Know that the Qur'ān is the ocean wherefrom the jewels of

1. The Arabic *Qirā'a* is used to mean both reading and reciting.

2. Bayhaqī, *Shu'ab al-Īmān,* 1865; Al-Shihāb, *Musnad,* 1284; al-Ḥakīm al-Tirmidhī, *Nawādir al-Uṣūl*, 3:255.

knowledge and the treasures of understanding are extracted. Any believer who is granted the way to understand it, his Opening [*Fatḥ*][3] becomes permanent, his light complete, his knowledge vast, and he never tires of reading it night and day, for he will have found therein his goal and purpose. This is the quality of the sincere disciple. Shaykh Abū Madyan—may God be pleased with him—has said, "A disciple is not a disciple until he is able to find in the Qur'ān everything that he desires."

Be careful to read those *sūras* and verses which are recommended in the *Sunna* at particular times; for example *al-Sajda* (The Prostration),[4] *al-Mulk* (The Kingdom),[5] *al-Wāqi'a* (The Event),[6] and the last two verses of *al-Baqara* (The Heifer)[7] every night before going to sleep; read *Al-Dukhān* (Smoke)[8] on Sunday and Thursday evenings and *al-Kahf* (The Cave)[9] on the nights before Mondays and Fridays. Read if you can the Seven Saving Ones[10] every night, for their merits are great. Also morning and evening the first few verses of *Sūra al-Ḥadīd* (Iron),[11] the last few verses of *Sūra al-Ḥashr* (The Mustering),[12] *Sūra al-Ikhlāṣ* three times and the two refuge-taking *sūras* three times each; similarly, *al-Ikhlāṣ* and the last two *sūras* together with the *al-Kursī* verse (The Footstool),[13] and *Sūra al-Kāfirūn* (The Disbelievers)[14] immediately before going to sleep, making these the last thing that you utter.

And God says the truth, and He guides to the way.

---

3. Opening (*fatḥ*): Victory in a general sense. The same word can be used for the conquest of a city, the dispelling of hardships, the achievement of success in any endeavor, and the unveiling of the Eye of the Heart, so that it begins to perceive the Unseen; it is usually in this latter sense that the term is used in Sufi texts.
4. Qur'ān, 32.
5. Qur'ān, 67.
6. Qur'ān, 56.
7. Qur'ān, 2.
8. Qur'ān, 44.
9. Qur'ān, 18.
10. The Seven Saving Ones are the following seven *Sūras*: *Al-Sajda* (The Prostration), *Ya-Sīn, Al-Dukhān* (Smoke), *Al-Wāqi'a* (The Event), *Al-Ḥashr* (The Gathering), *Al-Mulk* (Sovereignty), and *Al-Insān* (Man).
11. Qur'ān, 57.
12. Qur'ān, 59.
13. Qur'ān, 2:255.
14. Qur'ān, 109.

Chapter 7

On Acquiring Knowledge

You should have a *wird* of reading useful knowledge, which is that which increases your knowledge of the Essence of God, His Attributes, acts, and favors, makes you aware of his commands and prohibitions, leads you to detach yourself from the things of this world and desire only the hereafter, and brings the faults in your person, the defects in your acts, and the plots of your enemy to your notice. This knowledge is present in the Book, the *Sunna*, and the writings of the leading scholars. It was compiled by Imām al-Ghazālī in his highly valuable books. Those possessed of religious perspicacity, who are well steeped in knowledge, and who have complete certitude, have great esteem for his books. If you are resolved to travel the path and arrive at the levels of realization, you must make it a habit to read them. The Ghazālī books are unique among the writings of authoritative Sufis in that they are comprehensive, explicit, and greatly effective within a short time.

You must read extensively in books of *ḥadīth* and *tafsīr*[1] and those of the "People"[2] in general, for this is where, as a Knower once said, a comprehensive opening and complete travelling are to be found. However, you must be wary of whatever their treatises include by way of obscure matters and bare Realities. These are present in most of the writings of Shaykh Muḥyiddīn ibn 'Arabī, and a few of Imām al-Ghazālī's treatises such as *al-Mi'rāj* (The Ascent) and *al-Maḍnūni bih* (The Withheld). Shaykh

---

1. *Tafsīr* is Qur'ānic exegesis or commentary.

2. The "People" (*Al-Qawm*) is an expression used to designate the Sufis, particularly the masters among them. It was originally taken from a *Ḥadīth Qudsī* where the descent of angels upon gatherings of *dhikr* is described, with God's forgiveness embracing all present, including those who just happened to be there for incidental worldly reasons, because the people of *dhikr* are "*the people whose companions never suffer wretchedness*."

Zarrūq[3] warned about such books in his *Ta'sīs al-Qawā'id* (Setting the Foundations); you can read it if you wish. Although he did not mention the writings of Shaykh 'Abd al-Karīm al-Jīlī, for he was a latecomer, his writings should be avoided for the sake of safety. Should someone say, "There is no harm in reading such books, for I shall take that which I understand and leave well alone that which I do not," I would say, "You speak fairly; however, what we fear for you is that which you think you understand, but have understood incorrectly, thereby leading you away from the Straight Path, as has happened to some who were assiduous readers of those books, who ended up in heresy and unbelief, and talked about incarnation [*ḥulūl*] and union [*ittiḥād*]."[4]

There is neither ability nor power save by God the High, the Immense.

3. Shaykh Aḥmad ibn Aḥmad Abū al-'Abbās Zarrūq who hails from Fez in Morocco was a great Shādhilī Sufi master who is also a jurist and a traditionist. He studied in Egypt and Madina, wrote many well-known works on Sufism, and died near Misurata in Libya in 899 A.H.

4. *Ḥulūl* or incarnation is the concept of God becoming incarnate in a human body, a rationally untenable proposition, since we have here two entities, the greater one being required to be contained in the smaller. *Ittiḥād* or union means that two entities have united and become one, again a rationally impossible proposition. The two concepts have their origin in the incapacity of those not spiritually inclined to understand the Sufi state of *fanā'*.

Chapter 8

On Remembrance

You should have a *wird* of remembering God the Exalted [*dhikr*], to which you must set a limit with either a determined time or number. There is no harm in using a rosary to keep count.

Know that remembrance is, as a Knower once said, the pillar of the Path, the key to realization, the weapon to the disciple, and the unfolding of sainthood.

God the Exalted says, ***Remember Me and I shall remember you,***[1] and, ***Remember God while standing, sitting, and on your sides,***[2] and He says, Exalted is He, ***O believers, Remember God abundantly!***[3]

The Messenger of God—may blessings and peace be upon him—has said, *God the Exalted says, "I am as my Servant thinks of Me, and I am with him when he remembers Me. When he remembers Me within himself, I remember him within Myself; and when he remembers Me in a company, I remember him in a better company."*[4] And he has said, may peace be upon him, *God says, "I am the companion of him who remembers Me."*[5] And he has said, may peace be upon him, *Shall I inform you of the best of your actions, the purest in the sight of your Lord, and the most elevating to your degrees, that which is better for you than spending gold and silver, and than meeting your enemy so that you strike at their necks and they strike at yours*? They said, "Yes." And he said, *The remembrance of God.*[6]

Remembrance has fruits and consequences which those who

1. Qur'ān, 2:152.
2. Qur'ān, 4:103.
3. Qur'ān, 33:41.
4. Bukhārī, *Ṣaḥīḥ*, 7405; Muslim, *Ṣaḥīḥ*, 2675.
5. Paraphrase of the *ḥadīth* that says, *I am with My servant so long as he remembers Me and his lips move doing so,* in Bayhaqī, *Shu'ab al-Īmān,* 506; Ibn Ḥibbān, *Ṣaḥīḥ*, 815; Aḥmad, *Musnad*, 10976.
6. Tirmidhī, *Sunan*, 3377; Ibn Māja, *Sunan*, 3790.

persevere in it with good manners and attentiveness find. The least of these is to find it so sweet and pleasurable that every worldly pleasure becomes insignificant in comparison. The highest is to become extinct in the Remembered and absent to the remembrance itself as well as all else.

He who sits in a secluded place, in a state of purity, facing the *Qibla*, his limbs still and his head down, and then remembers God with an attentive heart and complete courtesy will see in his heart the manifest influence of the remembrance. If he perseveres, the lights of proximity descend upon his heart and the secrets of the unseen are unveiled.

The best remembrance is that which involves both the tongue and the heart. The remembrance of the heart is to be fully aware of the meaning of that which flows from the tongue, for example the meaning of transcendence and unification when one utters the words of glorification and unification [*tasbīḥ* and *tahlīl*].

When choosing between silent or vocal remembrance and recitation, the rule is: that what is better for the invoker is that which is more useful for his heart.

Remembrance is the continual, permanent *wird,* so strive to keep your tongue moist with it in all circumstances, except at those times where another *wird*—for example recitation or reflection—is due which cannot be done simultaneously. These and other devotions are, however, included in the more general sense of remembrance.

Do not confine yourself to only one kind of *dhikr*; rather, you should have a *wird* of every variety.

You must be careful to perform the textually transmitted invocations and prayers, those which follow the ritual prayers, those to be recited morning and evening, those before going to sleep and on waking up, and those with other specified times and recurrent occasions. The Messenger of God—may blessings and peace be upon him—made *Sunnas* of these only so that his community would find in them the means to obtain the good and escape the evil of such times and occasions. He who having neglected them suffers something he dislikes or is prevented from reaching his heart's desire should blame only himself. He who wishes to practice that which we have mentioned should consult Imām al-Nawawī's book, *al-Adhkār* (The Invocations); may God have mercy on him and reward him well on behalf of all Muslims. The best and most recommended of that which is reported to be following the ritual prayers is to say after each prescribed prayer, "*Allāhumma a'innī 'alā dhikrika wa shukrika wa ḥusni 'ibādatika*!" [O God! Help me to remember You, thank You, and worship You well!] and to recite the *tasbīh, taḥmīd,* and *takbīr* thirty-three times each, and to complete the count to a hundred by saying, "*Lā ilāha illa'llāhu waḥdahu lā sharīka lahu, lahul-mulku wa lahul-ḥamdu, wa huwa 'alā kulli shay'in qadīr.*" [There is no god save God alone, He has no partners, His is sovereignty, and His is all praise, and He has power to do all things.] Repeat this sentence ten times after the dawn, afternoon and sunset prayers, before moving your legs and before talking, and add to it, "*yuḥyi wa-yumīt,*" [He gives life and He gives death] after *lahul-ḥamdu.* Say also morning and evening, "*Subḥān Allāhi, wal-ḥamdu lil'llāhi, wa lā ilāha illa'llāhu, wal-llāhu akbar,*" [Transcendent is God, all praise belongs to God, there is no god but God, and God is Greater], one hundred times, and, "*Lā ilāha illa'llāhu waḥdahu lā sharīka lahu, lahul-mulku, wa lahul-ḥamdu, wa huwa 'alā kulli shay'in qadīr*" one hundred times each day.

Adopt a *wird* of invocations of blessings upon the Messenger of God—may blessings and peace be upon him—for this will be a connection between you and God's Beloved, and a door through which assistance from his presence flows in abundance to you. He has said—may blessings and peace be upon him and his family, *He who blesses me once, him shall God bless ten times.*[7] And, *The nearest to me on Resurrection Day are those who bless me the most.*[8] God exhorts you to do this in His August Book when He says, ***O believers, bless him and emphatically salute him,***[9] so obey and do it in abundance; add salutations [*salām*]; and include his family. In particular, repeat it frequently on Thursday nights and Fridays, for he has said, may peace be upon him, *Increase*

7. Ṭabarānī, *Awsaṭ*, 4948; Ibn al-Sunnī, *'Amal al-Yawm wa'l-Layla*, 380; Abū Ya'lā, *Musnad*, 4002; Abū Nu'aym, *Ḥilyat al-Awliyā'*, 4: 347.

8. Bayhaqī, *Ma'rifat al-Sunan wa al-Āthār,* 6672; *Shu'ab al-Īmān,* 2773; Bazzār, *Musnad,* 1789; Abū Ya'lā, *Musnad,* 5080.

9. Qur'ān, 33:56.

your invocations of blessings upon me in the White Night and the Bright Day.[10] May God bless him and his family, and grant them peace.

Praise belongs to God, Lord of the Worlds.

10. Bayhaqī, *Shu'ab al-Īmān,* 2772; Ṭabarānī, *Awsaṭ*, 241.

Chapter 9

On Reflection

You should have a *wird* of reflection in every twenty-four hours, for which you should set aside one or more hours. The best time for reflection is that in which are the least pre-occupations, worries, and the most potential for the heart to be present, such as the depth of the night. Know that the good of both one's religious and worldly affairs depends upon the soundness of one's reflection. He who is given a share of it has an abundant share of everything good. It has been said, "An hour's reflection is better than a year's worship". 'Alī—may God honor his face—has said, "There is no worship like reflection." And a Knower—may God have mercy on them all—said, "Reflection is the lamp of the heart; should it depart, the heart will possess no light."

The ways of reflection are many; the most noble is to reflect on the wonders of God's dazzling creation, the inward and outward signs of His ability, and the signs He has scattered abroad in the Realm of the earth and the heavens. This kind of reflection increases your knowledge of the Essence, Attributes, and Names of God. He encourages it by saying, ***Say, look at what is in the heavens and the earth!***[1]

Reflect on the wonders involved in His creation of you. He says, Exalted is He, ***In the earth are signs for those who have certainty, and in yourselves; can you not see?***[2]

Know that you must reflect on the favors of God and His bounties which He causes to reach you.

He says, Exalted is He, ***Remember the favors of God that you may succeed.***[3] ***Should you count the favors of God, you would be unable to number them.***[4] And He says, Exalted is He, ***All the***

1. Qur'ān, 10:10.
2. Qur'ān, 51:20, 21.
3. Qur'ān, 7:69.
4. Qur'ān, 45:18.

good things that you possess are from God.[5]

This kind of reflection results in the heart filling with the love of God, and continuously rendering thanks to Him, inwardly and outwardly, in a manner that pleases and satisfies Him.

Know that you should reflect on God's complete awareness of you, and His seeing and knowing all about you.

And He says, Exalted is He, ***We have created man, and We know what his soul whispers to him; and We are nearer to him than his jugular vein.***[6]

And He says, Exalted is He, ***And He is with you wherever you are; and God sees what you do.***[7]

And He says, Exalted is He, ***Have you seen that God knows what is in the heavens and the earth, and no three [persons] converse but that He is their fourth?***[8]

This kind of reflection results in your feeling ashamed before God should He see you where He has forbidden you to be, or miss you where He has commanded you to be.

Know that you must reflect on your shortcomings in worshipping your Lord, and exposing yourself to his wrath should you do what He has forbidden you.

God the Exalted says, ***I created men and jinn only to worship Me.***[9] ***Do you think that We created you in vain and that to us you will not be returned?***[10] ***O man, what is it that has deceived you concerning your Generous Lord?***[11]

And He says, Exalted is He, ***O man, you shall toil toward your Lord strenuously until you meet Him.***[12]

This kind of reflection increases your fear of God and encourages you to blame and reproach yourself, avoid remissness, and persevere in your zeal.

And know that you must reflect on this worldly life, its numerous preoccupations and hazards, and the swiftness with which

5. Qur'ān, 46:53.
6. Qur'ān, 1:16.
7. Qur'ān, 58:7.
8. Qur'ān, 58:7.
9. Qur'ān, 51:56.
10. Qur'ān, 23:115.
11. Qur'ān, 82:6.
12. Qur'ān, 84:16.

it perishes, and on the hereafter, and its felicity and permanence.

God the Exalted says, ***Thus does God render the signs clear to you that you may reflect on this world and the hereafter.***[13] And He says, Exalted is He, ***But you prefer the life of the world, when the hereafter is better and more abiding.***[14] And He says, Exalted is He, ***The life of this world is but distraction and play, while the last abode is indeed the Life, if but they knew.***[15]

This kind of reflection results in losing all desire for the world, and in wishing for the hereafter.

And know that you should reflect on the imminence of death and the regret and remorse which occur when it is too late.

God the Exalted says, ***Say: The death that you flee will indeed meet you; you will then be returned to the Knower of the unseen and the seen, and He will inform you of that which you have been doing.***[16] And He says, Exalted is He, ***Until, when death comes to one of them he says: "My lord, send me back that I may do good in that which I have left!" No! It is but a word he says.***[17] And He says, Exalted is He, ***O believers, let not your wealth or your children distract you from the remembrance of God!*** up to, ***but God will not reprieve a soul whose time has come.***[18]

The benefit of this kind of reflection is that hopes become short, behavior better, and provision is gathered for the Appointed Day.

Know that you should reflect on those attributes and acts by which God has described His friends and His enemies, and on the immediate and delayed rewards which He has prepared for each group.

God the Exalted says, ***The righteous are in felicity and the***

---

13. Qur'ān, 2:220.
14. Qur'ān, 77:17
15. Qur'ān, 29:64.
16. Qur'ān, 62:8.
17. Qur'ān, 23:99.
18. ***O believers, let not your wealth or your children distract you from the remembrance of God; those who do so are the losers. And spend of that which We have provided you with before death comes to one of you and he says, "My Lord, if only You would reprieve me for a little while, then I would give charity and be among the virtuous." But God will not reprieve a soul whose time has come, and God is aware of what you do.*** [Qur'ān, 63:9, 10, 11].

depraved are in Hell.[19]

And He says, Exalted is He, ***Is the one who is a believer like the one who is corrupt? They are not equal.***[20]

And He says, Exalted is He, ***As for the one who gave away, was God-fearing, and believed in goodness, We shall ease him into ease,***[21] up to the end of the *sūra*.

And He says, Exalted is He, ***The believers are those who, when God is mentioned, their hearts tremble,*** up to, ***they will have degrees with their Lord, and forgiveness and generous provision.***[22]

And He says, Exalted is He, ***God has promised those among you who have believed and done good works that He will make them rulers over the earth as He made those before them rulers.***[23]

And He says, Exalted is He, ***Each We took for their sin; on some We sent a hurricane, some were taken by the Cry, some We caused the earth to swallow, and some We drowned. It was not for God to wrong them, but they wronged themselves.***[24]

And He says, Exalted is He, ***Hypocrite men and women proceed one from another; they enjoin evil and forbid good,*** up to: ***God curses them, and theirs is a lasting torment.***[25]

And He says, Exalted is He, ***Believing men and women are helping friends to each other; they enjoin good and forbid evil,*** up to: ***and good pleasure from God which is greater; that is the supreme gain.***[26]

---

19. Qur'ān, 82:13, 14.
20. Qur'ān, 32:18.
21. Qur'ān, 42:5, 6, 7.
22. Qur'ān, 8:2, 3, 4.
23. Qur'ān, 24:55.
24. Qur'ān, 39:40.
25. ***Hypocrite men and hypocrite women proceed from one another; they enjoin evil and forbid good, and they withhold their hands. They forget God, so He forgets them. Indeed, the hypocrites are the corrupt. God promises the hypocrites, both men and women, and the disbelievers the fire of Hell for their abode; it will suffice them. God curses them, and theirs is a lasting torment.*** [Qur'ān, 9:67, 6]
26. ***Believing men and women are allies to each other. They enjoin good and forbid evil, correctly perform the prayer, give the*** **Zakāt**, ***and obey God and His Messenger. God will have mercy on them; He is indeed August, Wise. God has promised believing men and believing women gardens underneath which rivers flow, perpetually to abide therein, and pleasant dwellings in Gardens of***

And He says, Exalted is He, ***Those who do not expect to meet Us are content with the life of this world and feel secure therein,*** up to, ***and the end of their prayer shall be, "Praised be God, the Lord of the Worlds!"***[27]

The result of this kind of reflection is that you come to love the fortunate,[28] habituating yourself to emulate their behavior and take on their qualities, and detest the wretched,[29] habituating yourself to avoid their behavior and traits of character.

Were we to allow ourselves to pursue the various channels of reflection we would have to forgo the brevity which we intend. That which we have mentioned should suffice any reasonable person.

You should bring to mind with each kind of reflection those verses, *ḥadīths*, and other narratives relating to it. We have given an example of this by quoting some of the verses related to each kind of reflection.

Beware of reflecting on the Essence of God the Exalted or His Attributes, in the wish to understand their nature and how they exist. No one ever became enamored of this without falling into the abysses of neutralization [*ta'ṭīl*] or the traps of anthropomorphism [*tashbīḥ*].[30] The Messenger of God—may God's blessings and

---

Eden, and Good Pleasure from God, which is greater; that is the supreme gain. [Qur'ān, 9:71, 72]

27. ***Those who do not expect to meet Us are content with the life of this world and feel secure therein, and those who are heedless of Our signs, their refuge is the Fire, for what they have been earning. Indeed, those who believe and do deeds of righteousness, their Lord will guide them for their belief; beneath them will rivers flow in gardens of bliss; their prayer therein will be, "Transcendent are You O God!" And their greeting will be one of peace, and the end of their prayer will be, "Praise is all God's, the Lord of the Worlds!"*** [Qur'ān, 10:7, 8, 9, 10]

28. The fortunate are those whose destiny it is to be believers, behave in ways pleasing to God, and whose ultimate fate is salvation.

29. The wretched are those whose destiny it is to be disbelievers, either throughout their lives or, because of their corruption, at the instant of death, and who are therefore damned.

30. *Ta'ṭīl* or Neutralization is literalism in attributing transcendence to God to the extent of cancelling out the qualities He attributes to Himself in revealed scripture. The other extreme, *Tashbīḥ* or Anthropomorphism, is literalism in attributing to the Absolute qualities that can belong only to created beings, such as

peace be upon him—has said, *Reflect on the signs of God, but do not reflect on God,*[31] for you will never be able to give Him his due.

This is what we wished to explain concerning the proprieties of these functions [*dhikr* and *fikr*].

The aim and spirit of *awrād* is presence with God, so aim for it. You will never reach it unless you travel its road, which is to perform the external activities while striving to be present with God. When you persevere in this, you become immersed in the lights of Proximity, and the sciences of direct knowledge overflow upon you, at which time your heart becomes wholly intent on God and presence becomes its nature and deeply ingrained quality. At that time you have to exert yourself to be attentive to created beings when you need to and you may not always be able to. Such a situation results in one becoming absent [from creation], engrossed [in the Creator], and extinct to anything that is not Him. It also leads to other states that are special to the People of God. The foundation of all this is perseverance in outward devotions and taking care to perform them well and with an effort to be attentive to God.

Beware of leaving a *wird* for fear of not being able to persevere in it; for this is foolishness. You should not do, in each period of time, whatever happens to suit your energy and free time; on the contrary, you should have a minimum that you perform, which you can add to whenever you feel energetic, but never fall below when you feel lazy.

Know that hastening to acts of goodness, being careful with acts of worship and persevering in obedience, constitute the way of the Prophets and Saints, both at the beginning and end of their affair, for they are the created beings with the most knowledge of God, and it is therefore not surprising that they are the most worshipful, obedient, and fearful of Him, August and Majestic is

---

hands, feet, or the act of actually sitting on His Throne. Both *Tashbīḥ* and *Ta'ṭīl* have been adopted by people whose thinking is handicapped by superficiality and intolerance of ambiguity so that for them things should be either black or white, whereas the reality of not only God, but also His creation is far more complicated than that.

31. Bayhaqī, *Shu'ab al-Īmān,* 119; Ṭabarānī, *Awsaṭ*, 6319.

He. The attentiveness of a servant is equal to his love for his Lord. Love is consequent upon knowledge; in as much as a servant of God grows more knowledgeable of Him, so also shall he love Him more and worship Him more abundantly. If you become too busy amassing worldly things and following passions to have *awrād* and keep to acts of worship, strive to give your Lord an hour at the beginning and an hour at the end of each day when you occupy yourself with glorifying Him, asking forgiveness, and other kinds of devotions. It has been related that God the Exalted has said, "Son of Adam, dedicate to Me an hour at the beginning of your day and an hour at its end, and I will take care for you of all that lies in between." It has also been related that the record of a servant is shown to God at the end of each day, and, if at its beginning and end there is goodness, God the Exalted says to the angel, "Erase what is in between!" This is how gracious God is to us and to all people, but most people are not thankful.

Chapter 10

On Following the Book and Sunna

You must hold fast to the Book and the *Sunna*. Take refuge in them, for they are the upright religion of God and His straight path. Those who adhere to them find safety, profit, guidance, and protection; while those who deviate from them go astray, grieve, lose, and are broken. Let them govern you and control what you do, and consult them in your every affair, in obedience to the counsel of God and that of His Messenger. God the Exalted says, ***O believers, obey God and obey the Messenger, and those in authority among you. If you ever dispute concerning any matter, refer it to God and the Messenger,*** which means "refer it to the Book and *Sunna*."[1]

The Messenger of God—may God's blessings and peace be upon him—has said, *I bid you heed that which, if you hold to it firmly, will never err: the Book of God and my* Sunna.[2]

If it would please to you to be rightly-guided along the white road in which there is ***neither crookedness nor curvature,***[3] then measure all your intentions, traits of character, acts, and words against the Book and *Sunna*, and then retain whatever conforms to them, and abandon whatever does not. And always be cautious and follow the better alternative. Never innovate in religion, nor follow the ways of non-believers, for you will ***lose both this world and the hereafter, which thing is the manifest loss.***[4] Beware of novel things and contrived opinions, for he has said, may blessings and peace be upon him and his family, *Every addition is an*

1. Qur'ān, 4:59. The full passage runs as follows: ***O believers, obey God and obey the Messenger, and those in authority among you. If you ever dispute concerning any matter, refer it to God and the Messenger, if you believe in God and the Last Day. That is better and of fairer consequence.***

2. Bayhaqī, *al-Sunan al-Kubrā,* 20336, 20337; Bazzār, *Musnad,* 8993; Al-Ḥākim, *Mustadrak,* 318, 319; Dāraquṭnī, *Sunan*, 4606.

3. Qur'ān, 20:107.

4. Qur'ān, 22:11.

innovation, and every innovation is an error.[5] And, *He who adds to this affair of ours what does not belong to it is to be rejected.*[6]

There are three kinds of innovations. The first is a "good innovation," which is that which the well-guided leaders have opined in conformity with the Book and *Sunna*, intending to choose that which is more beneficial, more useful, and finer, as for example Abū Bakr's collection of the whole Qur'ān into one volume (*muṣhaf*), 'Umar's institution of military pensions and of the *Tarāwīḥ* prayers, 'Uthmān's arrangement of the Qur'ān and institution of a first Call to Prayer on Friday, and 'Alī's rules for fighting heretical rebels. May God bestow His good pleasure upon the four Caliphs. The second kind of innovation is one that is blameworthy only from the point of view of detachment and contentment, such as the lavish use of lawful clothes, foodstuffs, and houses. The third kind is the absolutely blameworthy innovation which contradicts the Book or *Sunna*, or the consensus of the community. Innovators have fallen into this very frequently with regards to principles [*uṣūl*], but infrequently with regard to branches [*furū'*]. Anyone who does not adhere to the utmost to the Book and *Sunna*, and does not do his best to emulate the Messenger, and then pretends that he has a degree in the sight of God the Exalted, should not be paid attention to, nor attended, even were he able to fly in the air, walk on water, have distances folded up, or the laws of nature broken for him. This does happen frequently with demons, magicians, soothsayers, diviners, astrologers, and others who are similarly in error. Such things can only be considered charismata [*karāmāt*] and confirmation, and not enticements and delusion, in the presence of rectitude [*istiqāma*] in the one upon whom they appear. Such deceivers can only deceive the rabble and the base people who worship God while harboring doubts. As for those endowed with reason and intelligence, they know full well that believers differ in their nearness to God according to the differences between them in following the Messenger, and the more complete the emulation, the more perfect the nearness to God and the greater the direct knowledge of Him. Abū Yazīd al-Bisṭāmī once went to visit a man who was said to be a saint. He sat

5. Abū Dāwūd, *Sunan*, 607; Nasa'ī, *Sunan*, 1578.
6. Bukhārī, *Ṣaḥīḥ*, 2697; Muslim, *Ṣaḥīḥ*, 1718.

down waiting for him in the mosque until the man came out and, feeling the need to spit, spat on the wall of the mosque, at which Abū Yazīd went away without speaking to him. He said, "How can one be entrusted with God's secret who is not careful to maintain the courtesies of the Law?" Junayd—may God have mercy on him—has said, "All roads are blocked except to him who follows in the footsteps of the Messenger, may blessings and peace be upon him." And Sahl ibn 'Abd Allāh [al-Tustarī]—may God have mercy on him—has said, "There is no helper but God, no guide but the Messenger of God, may God's blessings and peace be upon him, no provision but God-fearing, and no work but to bear the latter with fortitude."

Know that not everyone is capable of independently evaluating all his affairs, outward and inward, against the Book and the *Sunna*, for only erudite scholars can do this. Should you ever find difficulty doing so, go to one of those whom God commands you to have recourse to in His saying, Exalted is He, ***So ask the people of remembrance if you do not know.***[7] The "people of remembrance" are those who have knowledge of God and His religion, practice what they know for His sake, have no desire for the world, are not distracted by commerce from His remembrance,[8] summon to Him clear-sightedly,[9] and are those to whom His secrets are unveiled. The presence of such a one on the face of the earth has become so rare that some great men have gone so far as to say they no longer exist. The truth is that they do exist, but because of the unawareness of the élite[10] and the turning away of the commonalty, God has hidden them under the cloak of His possessiveness and surrounded them with veils of obscurity. However, those who seek them with sincerity and zeal will not—

7. Qur'ān, 16:43.

8. ***Men whom neither commerce nor transactions distract from the remembrance of God, from correctly performing the prayer and giving the* Zakāt, *who fear a day when hearts and eyes shall be turned about.*** [Qur'ān, 24:37]

9. ***Say: This is my way, I summon to God clear-sightedly, I and those who follow me.*** [Qur'ān, 12:108]

10. The élite in question is that of the scholarly community that is responsible for guiding the commonalty. Their unawareness, however, was said by *Ḥabīb* Aḥmad Mash'hūr al-Ḥaddād to be in no wise reprehensible, since it is imposed on them by the Real because of the particular pattern of the times.

by God's Will—fail to find one of them, for sincerity is a sword that is never used against anything without cutting it. The earth is never without those who uphold the matter for God. And he has said, may blessings and peace be upon him and his family, *There will always remain a group in my community who will defend the truth victoriously, unharmed by those who oppose them, until comes the command of God.*[11] These are the stars of the earth,[12] the carriers of the Trust, the deputies of the Chosen One, and the heirs of the Prophets. ***God is well-pleased with them and they are well pleased with Him***.[13] ***Those are God's faction; indeed, God's faction is those who will succeed.***[14]

---

11. Abū Dāwūd, *Sunan*, 2484; Aḥmad, *Musnad*, 19850. The meaning of the *ḥadīth* is that those who oppose these people will never be able to stamp out the light of Islam of which they are the custodians. As to harm coming to them personally, that has been a fairly frequent occurrence, as evidenced by what befell Imām Aḥmad ibn Ḥanbal—may God be pleased with him—and many others.

12. The Prophet—may blessings and peace be upon him—repeatedly declared that just as the stars were the security of the inhabitants of the sky, he was the security of his Companions, and that they in turn were the security of the people of the earth.

13. Qur'ān, 5:119.

14. Qur'ān, 58:22

Chapter 11

On Doctrine

You must correct and protect your beliefs in conformity with the pattern of the party of salvation, who is known among the other Islamic factions as the "People of the *Sunna* and *Jamā'a*." They are those who firmly adhere to the way of the Messenger of God, may blessings and peace be upon him, and his Companions.[1]

If you look with upright understanding and a sound heart into those passages relating to the sciences of faith in the Book, the *Sunna*, and the sayings of the virtuous predecessors, who are the Companions and the Followers, you will know for certain that the truth is with the party called the Ash'arīs, named after Shaykh Abū al-Ḥasan al-Ash'arī,[2] may God have mercy on him, who systematized the foundations of the creed of the people of the truth, and recorded its earliest version, these being the beliefs which the Companions and the best among the Followers agreed upon. These constitute the doctrine of the people of truth in every time and place, and of most of the Sufis, as Abū al-Qāsim al-Qushayrī—may God have mercy on him—indicated at the beginning of his *Risāla* or Treatise. It is—may God be praised—our doctrine, and that of our Ḥusaynī brothers known as the family of Abū 'Alawī, and of our predecessors from the time of the Messenger of God—may blessings and peace be upon him—down to the present day. When the Imām, the Emigrant to God, the ancestor of the said *sayyids*, my master Aḥmad ibn 'Īsā ibn Muḥammad ibn 'Alī ibn Ja'far al-Ṣādiq,[3] may God be pleased with them,

1. There are several *ḥadīths* stating that the community will divide into many different groups, all astray save one, defined by the Prophet—may blessings and peace be upon him—as, *those who are according to how I and my Companions are.* Tirmidhī, *Sunan*, 2641; Ṭabarānī, *Kabīr,* 62, 14646.

2. The Ash'arīs are the Followers of the principal school of orthodox Muslim theology founded by Abū al-Ḥasan al-Ash'arī. (d. 935 C.E.)

3. Imām Aḥmad ibn 'Īsā al-Muhājir was one of the most knowledgeable and saintly members of the House of the Prophet, may blessings and peace be

saw how innovations had appeared, passions multiplied, and opinions diverged in Iraq, he emigrated and travelled the earth until he reached the land of Ḥaḍramaut where he stayed until his death. And God blessed his descendants, a great many of whom became renowned for their knowledge, worship, sainthood, and direct knowledge. Through the *baraka* of this trustworthy Imām who fled from sedition to protect his religion, they remained safe from the innovations and misguided passions into which certain other factions of the Prophetic House had fallen. May God reward him on our behalf with the best reward He has ever granted a father on behalf of his children; may He raise his degree along with his noble forefathers in the Highest Heaven [*'Illiyūn*] and give us to join them in goodness and safety, having neither changed our religion nor fallen into temptation. He is the Most Merciful. The Māturīdīs[4] are the same as the Ash'arīs in the above regard.

Each believer must protect his faith by learning the creed of one of the Imāms who are incontestably worthy of respect and well-grounded in knowledge. And I can see none more clear, comprehensive, and free from suspect and misleading things than that of Imām al-Ghazālī, may God be pleased with him. This is to be found in the first chapter of the volume on the foundations of beliefs in the *Iḥyā'*.[5] Should you wish for more then look into the

---

upon him. His title *al-Muhājir,* the Emigrant, meant primarily that he had forsaken the world and traveled the path to God, and secondarily that he had emigrated from Iraq to Ḥaḍramaut where his descendants became the illustrious 'Alawī *sādat.* When he reached Ḥaḍramaut in about 318 A.H, the land was poor, unsafe, and dominated by the Ibāḍiyya, an extremist sect. He summoned the people to God, established the *Sunna,* and adopted the Shāfi'ī School of law. He died in 345 A.H. having lived about a hundred years.

4. Māturīdīs are the followers of the second largest orthodox Muslim theological school, that of Abū Manṣūr al-Māturīdī. (d. 944 C.E.), today confined largely to Turkey, the Turkestan, and the Indian subcontinent.

5. *Iḥyā' 'Ulūm al-Dīn: The Revival of the Religious Sciences.* The main work of Ghazālī and one of the most important and comprehensive books in the history of Islam. It is still, nine centuries later, in print in every single Muslim country in the world. It is in four volumes, the first containing the Islamic creed, the nature of knowledge, and a detailed description of the forms and secrets of each act of worship. The second is concerned with transactions, whether on the personal, social, commercial, or political level. The last two volumes are about virtues and ridding oneself of unwanted attributes, both of which endeavors are

Jerusalem Epistle (*Al-Risāla al-Qudsiyya*) in the third chapter of the same book.

Do not delve too deeply into theology [*Kalām*], nor discuss it much if your aim is acquiring direct knowledge [*ma'rifa*], for it cannot be obtained through that science. If you want to acquire this kind of knowledge, you must travel its path, which is to adhere to God-fearing outwardly and inwardly, meditate on verses and *ḥadīths*, reflect on the Realm of the heaven and the earth with the aim of drawing lessons, refine the soul's attributes, reduce its densities through discipline, polish the mirror of the heart by continual remembrance [*dhikr*] and reflection [*fikr*], and by shunning everything that might distract you from devoting yourself entirely to this affair. This is the way to attain, and if you tread it you will—by God's will—find what you are seeking. Sufis struggle against their souls, discipline them and wean them of their habits and familiar things, because they know that on this depends the fullness of direct knowledge, and on the fullness of direct knowledge depends the realization of the Station of Servitude ['*ubūdiyya*] which is the goal of the Knowers and the hope of those who realize, may God be pleased with them.

---

necessary for any traveler on the Sufi path. The third volume deals with "Ruinous Things," such as greed, avarice, ostentation, and pride, and the fourth with "Saving Things" such as hope, fear, sincerity, fortitude, etc. The book is so detailed and thorough that it may, in the opinion of many Sufi Shaykhs, be used as a guide on the path in the absence of a guiding Shaykh.

Chapter 12

On Religious Obligations

You must observe both the obligations and the prohibitions, and increase your supererogatory devotions. For if you do this purely for the sake of God you will attain to the utmost proximity to Him, the gift of love shall be bestowed upon you, and then all your movements and standstills will be for and by Him. This is the investiture of sainthood or even vice-regency [*khilāfa*].[1] And this is what the Messenger of God—may blessings and peace be upon him and on his family—was referring to when he said, *God the Exalted says, "My servant draws nearer to Me with nothing more pleasing to Me than what I have made obligatory upon him. He then continues to draw nearer to Me with supererogatory devotions until I love him; and when I love him, I become his hearing with which he hears, his sight with which he sees, his hand with which he grasps, and his foot with which he walks, so that by Me he hears, by Me he sees, by Me he grasps, and by Me he walks. Should he ask anything of Me, I shall surely grant it, and should he request protection, I shall surely protect him. Never do I hesitate as in taking the soul of My believing servant; he dislikes death and I dislike to displease him, but it is a thing inevitable."*[2]

See—may God have mercy on you—what this *Ḥadīth Qudsī* (Holy Tradition)[3] contains of secrets and inward wisdom, and ponder on the fine meanings and subtleties to which it alludes. This fortunate servant only reaches such a great rank, where ev-

---

1. *Khilāfa*: Vice-Regency, the status of one who has achieved utter extinction in the Real and thus become the perfect instrument for His government of creation. Used in the context of the material world it designates the succession to the rulership of the Muslim community following the death of the Prophet, may blessings and peace be upon him, starting with the four "Rightly Guided Successors" or Caliphs (*Khulafā'*): Abū Bakr, 'Umar, 'Uthmān, and 'Alī.

2. Bukhārī, *Ṣaḥīḥ*, 6502.

3. A *Ḥadīth Qudsī* or Holy Utterance consists of the words of God which have been reported by the Blessed Prophet, but are not part of the Qur'ān.

erything he likes is liked by God and everything he dislikes is disliked by Him, by virtue of his conforming to what He has made obligatory upon him, and his performing supererogatory devotions in abundance in his wish to draw nearer to Him. So make haste! Make haste if you are determined to reach the degrees of perfection and wish to attain to the ranks of men.[4] The path is now clear before you, and the radiance of realization has appeared to you.

And know that God—by His grace and mercy—has put much good into supererogatory devotions to make up for the many imperfections in obligatory ones. However, any imperfection in an obligatory act can only be redeemed by an act of supererogation of the same kind: prayer by prayer and fasting by fasting. Obligations are the basis and acts of supererogation secondary to them.

He who performs the obligations, avoids prohibited things, and does not add anything to this, is better off than he who performs acts of supererogation while neglecting some obligations. Beware, therefore, of neglecting any obligations while occupied with acts of supererogation, for you would thereby sin by abandoning your obligations, and your acts of supererogation would thereby become unacceptable to God. An example of this is a man who occupies himself with acquiring a kind of knowledge which is for him supererogatory, while neglecting to acquire another which is for him obligatory, either outwardly or inwardly. Another is a man who is able but neglects to work for a livelihood and busies himself with supererogatory devotions, leaving his family to beg from others. You can use these two examples to assess by analogy other similar situations.

Know that you will never attain to performing obligations, avoiding prohibited things, and performing the supererogatory acts that He has laid down for you to draw nearer to Him, save through knowledge. Seek it, then! For he has said, may blessings and peace be upon him and his family, *Seeking knowledge is an obligation to every Muslim.*[5] Knowledge makes you aware of what is a duty, what is recommended, what is forbidden, how to per-

4. A "Man" in Sufi terminology is one who has realized the virtues and become firmly established in sainthood.

5. Ibn Māja, *Sunan*, 224; Bazzār, *Musnad,* 94. Abū Ya'lā, *Musnad*, 2903.

form your duties and recommended acts, and how to avoid what is prohibited. Therefore, you must have knowledge and cannot dispense with it, for on the practice of it depends your happiness in this world and the next. Know that those who worship but have no knowledge end up receiving more harm from their worship than benefit. How many a worshipper has tired himself out in worshipping while persistently committing a sin which he believed to be an act of obedience or [at any rate] not a sin! The Knower Shaykh, Ibn 'Arabī, in the chapter on advice in the *Futūḥāt*, relates the story of a Moroccan who showed great zeal in worship, and [one day] bought a female donkey which he never [ostensibly] used for any purpose. A man questioned him about why he kept the animal and he replied, "I keep it to protect my genitals [from illegal intercourse]." He did not know that it was prohibited to have intercourse with animals! When he was informed of this, he was frightened and wept profusely.

The knowledge that is obligatory upon every Muslim is to know the mandatory status of everything God has made obligatory upon him, and the forbidden status of those which God has prohibited. As for knowing the way to perform each obligation, this becomes obligatory only at the time of wanting to perform it. The one who reaches puberty or enters Islam in the month of Muḥarram, for instance, must immediately learn the meaning of the Two Affirmations and utter them, and then learn about the duty of performing the five prayers and their necessary components and rules. He must then learn about the obligations of fasting, *Zakāt*, Pilgrimage, and so forth, and the prohibition of illegal intercourse, wine-drinking, the wrongful appropriation of other people's wealth, and the other things forbidden by the Law. It is not necessary for him to learn precisely how to fast until Ramaḍān, how to perform the Ḥajj until it is actually time for it, nor how to calculate the *Zakāt* until he has enough money for the *Zakāt* to become due and its time arrives. And God knows best.

The main duties and prohibitions are well known among Muslims; the important thing, however, is to know the various rules, which can only be acquired from a scholar who fears God and upholds the truth. Common people are sometimes right in their behavior and sometimes not, so beware of doing or refraining from doing as they do simply by emulation, for emulation is only sound if it is of a scholar who practices what he knows, and such people are today a rarity. Therefore, if you see a scholar these days and observe him doing or leaving something, and you do not know whether this is right or wrong, do not be content with just having seen what he does or refrains from doing; ask him about the legal reasons and the religious rules behind it.

A Muslim does not need a long time to acquire the knowledge that is obligatory for him, nor is much hardship involved. An intelligent student will find it sufficient to sit with a proficient scholar for an hour or two. A Bedouin once came to the Messenger of God—may God's blessings and peace be upon him and his family—while he was preaching from his pulpit and asked him to teach him some of that which God had taught him. He came down from the pulpit, taught him, then climbed back again and resumed his sermon.

On the whole, those who wish for both security and gain must not initiate any act or continue with something already initiated until they know God's ruling concerning it: whether it is obligatory, recommended, just licit, or prohibited. Everything will fall into one of these four groups. Surely this must be a duty for every Muslim.

Believers can be divided into the commonalty and the elect. The former may fall into neglecting duties and committing forbidden things and the best among them are those who hasten to repent and ask for forgiveness. They are not keen on supererogatory devotions and use the merely licit category to excess. As for the elect, they carry out their obligations and avoid prohibitions under all circumstances, are careful to perform the recommended things, and confine themselves when using the merely licit to that which is a means of conforming to [God's] orders and prohibitions. And God is the one who grants success.

Chapter 13

On Cleanliness

You must take good care of your cleanliness, both outward and inward, for he who is completely clean becomes inwardly and in spirit a spiritual angel, although he remains outwardly and in body a physical human being. The Messenger of God—may God's blessings and peace be upon him—has said, *Religion is based on cleanliness.*[1] And, *God is clean and likes cleanliness.*[2]

Inward cleanliness is achieved by purifying the soul from vile traits of character such as pride, ostentation, jealousy, love of the world, and other similar things, and adorning it with noble traits of character such as humility, modesty, sincerity, generosity, and so forth. The true nature of these and the way to rid oneself of vile traits and acquire noble ones was explained fully by Imām al-Ghazālī in the second half of the *Iḥyā'*. Know this and make use of it!

As for outward cleanliness, this depends on avoiding transgressions and keeping to obedience.

He who adorns his outward with perseverance in good works and his inward with acquiring praiseworthy attributes has completed his cleanliness. Otherwise, he would only have a share of it proportionate to his remoteness from reprehensible traits and acts, and nearness to good ones.

Among the kinds of outward cleanliness are those things indicated in the Law, such as the removal of excessive hair, and of nails and dirt, and the purification from impurities and acts which necessitate ritual ablution. Amongst these are the removal of pubic hair, depilation or shaving of the armpits, clipping the moustache and paring the fingernails. It is recommended to start with the right index finger, carry on to the right little finger, then the left little finger, through to the left thumb, and end with the right

1. Suyūṭī, *al-Jāmi' al-Ṣaghīr wa Ziyādātuh,* 6234.
2. Tirmidhī, *Sunan*, 2799.

thumb. As for the feet, one begins with the right little toe and ends with the left little toe, in the same order as washing between the toes during the ritual ablution [*wuḍū'*]. It is reprehensible to delay any of these beyond forty days. Other things are the removal with water of the dirt which accumulates between the body's wrinkles and folds, the mucus in the eyes, the dirt in the nostrils, and the removal with a toothpick what remains stuck between the teeth. You must clean your mouth with the *siwāk*, and it is better if it is of Arak wood; it is strongly recommended before initiating any act of worship. You must also wash your clothes with water whenever they become dirty, in moderation and without imitating those who live in luxury.

Other *Sunnas* related to cleanliness are perfuming and combing the beard, cleaning all hair, using *ithmid* kohl[3] thrice in each eye, for he used kohl—may peace be upon him—every night in this manner, using perfume in abundance, for it masks unpleasant odors, human or otherwise; this is firmly recommended for the Friday Prayer and other gatherings of Muslims. The Messenger of God—may God's blessings and peace be upon him and his family—liked it and used it abundantly; sometimes the shine of perfume would be seen on the parting of his hair. This he did so that others would imitate him, for his body was naturally fragrant; he was in no need of perfume, and they used to collect his perspiration to use as perfume. It is good for men to use perfume with a strong scent but no color, and for women the opposite.

Beware of all impure substances. If soiled by any such substance that is damp, wash it out as soon as possible. If you become impure [*junub*] due to sexual intercourse, perform the greater ablution [*ghusl*] immediately, for the *junub* is forbidden from the presence of God, which is why he is forbidden to stay in the mosque or recite the Qur'ān. It has been said that the angels do not enter a house where there is a *junub* person, and when the angels go the devils arrive from every direction. Beware of eating or sleeping while *junub*, for you would thus expose yourself to many problems; if it is not possible for you to take an immediate *ghusl*, then the least you can do is to wash your private parts and perform *wuḍū'*.

3. *Ithmid* is the best kind of kohl known to the Arabs to this day.

You should renew your *wuḍū'* before each obligatory prayer and strive always to remain in a state of ritual purity. Renew your *wuḍū'* whenever you break it, for it is the weapon of the believer and when the weapon is in evidence, the enemy dares not approach.

A man once came to Shaykh Abū al-Ḥasan al-Shādhilī—may God be pleased with him—and asked him to teach him alchemy. The Shaykh promised to teach him, but only after he had stayed with him for a year and on condition that each time he broke his *wuḍū'* he would renew it and pray two *rak'as*. At the end of the year the man went to draw water from a well and the bucket came up full of gold or silver. He poured it all back into the well, for he had no desire for it whatsoever, then he went to the Shaykh and told him. The Shaykh replied, "You have now become all alchemy." And he made him a summoner to God the Exalted.

Pray two *rak'as* each time you make *wuḍū'*. If you cannot remain continually ritually pure try always being so whenever you are sitting in the mosque, reciting the Qur'ān, acquiring knowledge, sitting for *dhikr*, or engaged in any other devotion.

When you make *wuḍū'* or *ghusl* beware of confining yourself to what is obligatory. On the contrary, you should take care to perform all the relevant *Sunnas* and proprieties, in the manner that has been handed down to you regarding his *ghusl* and *wuḍū'*—may peace be upon him.

You should perform *ghusl* every now and then with the intention of maintaining cleanliness, even if you are not *junub*. A *ghusl* on Friday is recommended in the *Sunna* for those who attend the Friday Prayer, and you should perform this, which, under some circumstances and for some people, should suffice for cleanliness.

When you finish your *wuḍū'* or *ghusl* say, "*Ash-hadu an lā ilāha illa'llāhu waḥdahu lā sharīka lahu wa ash-hadu anna Muḥammadan 'abduhu wa rasūluh.*" [I testify that there is no divinity but God alone, He has no partners, and I testify that Muḥammad is His servant and Messenger.][4]

---

4. 'Uqba ibn 'Āmir said, "We took turns guarding the camels. When it was my turn and I brought them back in the evening, I found the Messenger of God—may God's blessings and peace be upon him—still standing up talking and I was able to hear him say, *No Muslim shall make* wuḍū' *in a thorough manner, and*

Chapter 14

On Following the Sunna

Adhere to the good manners of the *Sunna* outwardly and inwardly; in both habitual and devotional activities; and you will have perfected your following and emulation of the Messenger of God, Messenger of Mercy, and Prophet of Guidance.

If it would please you to become one of the Veracious [*Ṣiddīqūn*], do not initiate any kind of habitual, let alone devotional behavior, until you study it and ascertain whether the Messenger of God—may God's blessings and peace be upon him—or any of his leading Companions thus behaved. If you find that they did not, although able to, then refrain, even if it be something licit, for they refrained from it only because of their knowledge that to do so was better. If you find that they did it, find out how they did it, and then follow suit. A certain scholar who refrained from eating watermelon explained his behavior by saying that he had been informed that the Prophet—may blessings and peace be upon him—had eaten it, but had not been informed in which manner, so he abstained from it.

We have mentioned previously and will again mention later on, God willing, some of the good manners to be observed during devotional activities. In this chapter we shall mention some of the good manners to be observed during everyday activities. Know that the one who observes the Prophetic good manners in his everyday activities is preserved by God from trespassing into base attributes or behavior and obtains both the worldly and religious

---

then rise to pray two rak'as *with full concentration of the heart and face, but that he will have deserved the Garden.* I said, "How generous is this!" Someone said, "The previous one was even more generous." I looked up and there was 'Umar, who added, "I saw you coming in just now. He has also said, *None of you shall make* wuḍū' *in a thorough manner, and then say*, Ash-hadu an lā ilāha illa'llāhu waḥdahu lā sharīka lahu wa ash-hadu anna Muḥammadan 'abduhu wa rasūluh, *but that the eight gates of the Garden shall open before him for him to enter from whichever he may wish.* [Muslim, *Ṣaḥīḥ*, 234.]

benefits that God has placed, in His wisdom, within these habitual activities.

He whom it would please to become completely free and clean from impurities and selfish human passions should make all his motions and stillnesses outwardly, and inwardly conform to the Sacred Law and follow the dictates of both Law and reason. Whenever the Sufis deprecate certain everyday activities, their purpose is the manner in which these are done, for instance under the influence of cravings and passions, to excess, or without preservation of the good manners prescribed by the Law. The Proof of Islam said in *Al-Arba'īn Al-Aṣl* [*The Forty Foundations*], after providing encouragement to follow the Prophet and pointing out certain of the secrets of this, "All this applies to everyday activities. As for acts of worship, I know of no cause for leaving the *Sunna* that is not begotten of either concealed disbelief or manifest foolishness; so know this!"

Know that you should begin everything you do with the Name of God; if you forget the Name at the beginning, say when you remember, "In the Name of God at its beginning and its end."

Try never to do anything habitual without first forming a good intention. When you put on your clothes, intend to cover the parts that God has ordered you to cover. Put on the right sleeve of shirts and similar garments first, and take it off last. Do not allow the cloth you wrap on the lower half of your body or your shirt to go further down than the middle of your shin; if you must, then no lower than the ankle. Women are allowed to let their dresses down to the ground on all sides but not to let them trail more than two-thirds of a cubit. Shorten the sleeves of your shirt to the wrist or the fingertip; if you do lengthen it beyond, then without excess.[1] The sleeve of the shirt of the Messenger of God—may blessings and peace be upon him—was down to his wrist, and 'Alī shortened the sleeves of his shirt to the fingertips. Acquire only such clothes as you need to wear and seek neither the most luxurious, nor the coarsest of clothes, but adhere to moderation. Do not expose the areas that must be kept covered or any part of them except when necessary. When it becomes necessary to do

1. People seem to have been lengthening their sleeves and upturning them as a show of affluence.

so, say before proceeding, "*Bismillāhi' lladhī lā ilāha illā hu*" [In the Name of God, who is the only deity].[2] When you put on your clothes say, "*Alḥamdu li'llā'hi'lladhī kasānī hādhā ath-thawba warazaqanīhi min ghayri ḥawlin minnī wa-lā quwwa*" [Praised and thanked be God, who clothed me in this garment and granted it me without any ability or power on my part].[3] It is *Sunna* to wear a turban, but not to make one's sleeves too wide, nor the turban too large.

You must utter only words of goodness. Everything that is forbidden to say is forbidden to listen to. When you speak, do so clearly and methodically, listen to what is being said to you, and interrupt no-one except when what is being said is abhorrent to God—backbiting, for instance. Beware of speaking in a disorderly manner. If someone says something to you that you already know, do not make him aware that you know it, for it will make your companion feel estranged. If someone relates a story or anything else to you inaccurately, do not say to him, "It is not as you say, it is like this and this." If the subject is religious, inform him of the correct version, but gently. Beware of delving into that which does not concern you or of swearing by God too frequently. Do not swear by Him—Transcendent and Exalted is He—except truthfully and when strictly necessary. Beware of all kinds of lying, for it is incompatible with faith. Beware of backbiting and tale-bearing, and of excessive levity. Avoid all other kinds of ugly talk and refrain from unseemly, just as you refrain from frankly blameworthy, speech. Think about what you are about to say before you say it; if it is good, go ahead, but if not, keep silent. He has said, may blessings and peace be upon him and his family, *Everything that the son of Adam says is against, not for him, except the remembrance of God, enjoining good, or forbidding evil.*[4] And he has said, may blessings and peace be upon him and his family, *May God have mercy on a man who says words of goodness and thus profits, or refrains from saying evil and thus is safe.*[5] And he has said, may blessings and peace be upon him and

2. Ibn al-Sunnī, *'Amal al-yawm wa'l-layla*, 273.
3. Abū Dāwūd, *Sunan*, 4023; Dārimī, *Musnad*, 2732.
4. Abū Dāwūd, *Sunan*, 4023; Ibn Māja, *Sunan*, 3974.
5. Ibn Abī al-Dunyā, *Kitāb al-Samt*, 64; Ibn al-Mubārak, *Kitāb al-Zuhd*, 380.

his family, *A man may utter a word that angers God, thinking it insignificant, yet it leads him to plummet into Hell.*[6]

Walk only to something good or necessary, and when you do, do not be in too much of a hurry. Do not strut with conceit or vanity, thereby falling in God's esteem. Do not get annoyed if someone walks before you and do not become elated when people follow on your footsteps and walk behind you, for such are the attributes of the arrogant. Do not turn around excessively as you walk and do not stop just out of curiosity. The Prophet used to walk powerfully, may blessings and peace be upon him, as if going downhill, and when called, used to stop, but not turn around.

When you sit, take care to keep your private parts covered, face the *Qibla*, sit with reverence and gravity, and refrain from fidgeting, restlessness, and repeatedly getting up. Beware of excessively scratching, stretching, belching, and yawning in people's faces. If yawning overpowers you, cover your mouth with your left hand. Beware of laughing too often, for it kills the heart, and if you can convert your laughter into a smile, then do so. Do not rise from your seat before saying, "*Subḥānaka'llāhumma wa-biḥamdika, ash-hadu an lā ilāha illā anta, astaghfiruka wa-atūbu ilayk.*" [Transcendent are You, O God, and praised by Your praises, I bear witness that there is no god but You, I seek Your forgiveness and repent unto You.] For it has been handed down that whoever says so is forgiven anything he may have done while sitting.[7]

When you want to sleep lie down on your right side, facing the *Qibla*, repent from all your sins and intend to rise at night for worship. Say, "*Bismika'llāhumma rabbi waḍa'tu janbi wa-bismika arfa'uh, fa'ghfir lī dhanbi. Allāhumma qinī 'adhābaka yawma tajma'u 'ibādak.*" [In Your Name, O God, my Lord, do I rest my side, and in Your Name do I raise it, so forgive me my sin. O God, protect me from your chastisement on the day when You gather your servants] (three times). "*Astagfirullāh'al 'aẓimi'lladhī lā ilāha illā huwa'l-ḥayyu'l-qayyūmu wa-atūbu ilayh.*" [I seek God's forgiveness, the Immense with whom there is no other deity, the Living, the Sustainer; and I repent unto him]

6. Bukhārī, *Ṣaḥīḥ*, 6478.
7. Abū Dāwūd, *Sunan*, 4857; Tirmidhī, *Sunan*, 3433.

(three times). And: "*Subḥān Allāh*" (thirty-three times), "*Alḥamdu lil'lāh*" (thirty-three times), and "*Allāhu Akbar*" (thirty-four times). There are other invocations to be recited before sleep, which you should not neglect. Sleep only in a state of ritual purity and go to sleep remembering God the Exalted. Do not get used to comfortable beds, for they lead to too much sleep and the neglect of night vigils; you would then feel great sorrow and regret when you see that which God has prepared for those who rise at night. He has said, may blessings and peace be upon him and his family, *People will be assembled on one plain and a herald will call, "Where are those whose sides shunned their resting places?" They will rise and a few they shall be, and they shall enter the Garden without reckoning.*[8] And he has said, may blessings and peace be upon him and his family, *The mother of Solomon, son of David, said to him—may peace be upon them— "O my son, do not sleep much at night, for he who sleeps at night shall come a pauper on Resurrection Day!"*[9]

Imām al-Ghazālī—may God's mercy be upon him—says, "Know that a night and a day are twenty-four hours. Do not sleep more than eight, for it should suffice, were you to live sixty years, to have wasted twenty, for these are one third." If due to circumstances you find yourself unable simultaneously to sleep on your right side and face the *Qibla*, then sleep on your right side and try not to give your back to the *Qibla*. If you lie down to rest but not to sleep, there is no harm in lying on your left side. A midday nap helps you to rise at night, and you should therefore take one. Beware of sleeping either after the Morning Prayer, for this stops provision [from reaching you], or after the Afternoon Prayer, for this results in insanity, or yet before the Night Prayer, for this conduces to insomnia. If you see something in a dream that pleases you, thank God and interpret it in an appropriate and goodly way, for in this manner it will be fulfilled. When you see something dis-

---

8. Bayhaqī, *Shu'ab al-Īmān,* 2974. *Those whose sides shunned their resting places* are those mentioned in the following verses: ***Those believe in Our signs who, when they are reminded of them, fall into prostration, extol the praises of their Lord, and are not arrogant. Their sides shun their resting places, they pray to their Lord in fear and hope, and of what We have provided them they freely spend.*** [Qur'ān, 31:15, 16]

9. Ibn Māja, *Sunan,* 1332; Bayhaqī, *Shu'ab al-Īmān,* 4417.

turbing, ask God for protection from evil, blow some spittle three times to your left, turn over to your other side, and speak about it to no-one, for in this manner it will not harm you. When someone relates a dream to you, do not interpret it unless either he asks you to or you ask him for his permission.

When you either eat or drink, always begin with *bismillāh* [in the Name of God] and conclude with *alḥamdu lil'lāh* [praised be God]. Eat and drink using your right hand. When food is offered to you, say, "*Allāhumma bārik lanā fīhi wa aṭ'imnā khayran minh*" [O God, bless what you have given us, and give us to eat that which is yet better]; if it be milk, however, you should say, "*wa zidnā minh*"[10] [and give us more of it], for there is nothing better, as has been handed down. Wash your hands before and after eating, eat small morsels, chew thoroughly, and do not extend your hand to more food before you have swallowed what is already in your mouth. Eat from the borders of the bowl, not from the middle, for the middle is where the *baraka* descends. If you drop a morsel, clean and then eat it, but do not leave it to the Devil. Lick your fingers and clean the bowl after you have finished. Use your index, middle finger, and thumb in eating; you can use the remaining fingers whenever you need to, for instance when eating rice. When you eat with others, partake of what is immediately before you, except when eating fruit. Do not keep looking at the other people who are eating; make appropriate conversation, and do not speak with food in your mouth. If you find it necessary to spit or blow your nose, turn your head away from them or go somewhere else. Whenever you eat at someone's house, praise him and pray for his felicity. Once you have finished eating, say, "*Al-ḥamdu lil'llāh, Allāhumma aṭ'amtanī ṭayyiban fasta'milnī ṣāliḥan; al-ḥamdu lil'llāhi'lladhī aṭ'amanī hādhal-ṭa 'āma wa-razaqanihi min ghayri ḥawlin minnī wa lā quwwa.*" [Praised be God! O God, You have fed me on goodness, therefore use me in goodness. Praised be God, Who fed me with neither ability nor power on my part.] The one who says this is forgiven his sins, past and future. Do not feel obliged to use sauce with every kind of

10. Abū Dāwūd, *Sunan,* 3730; Tirmidhī, *Sunan,* 3455.

food,[11] and never criticize food, however bad it is. Do not make good and pleasurable food your prime concern; otherwise, you will be one of those about whom the Messenger of God—may God's blessings and peace be upon him—said, *The worst among my community are those who eat luxurious food and their bodies grow on it. Their concern lies only in varying their food and clothes, and they speak pretentiously.*[12] 'Alī—may God honor his face—has said, "The one whose main concern is what enters his belly is worth that which comes out."

Strive to allow only lawful [*ḥalāl*] food to enter your stomach, for the heart of he who eats lawful food for forty days becomes illuminated and the wellsprings of wisdom flow from his tongue, God honors him with detachment from the world, his inward becomes clear, and his behavior towards his Lord excellent. On the other hand, he who eats suspect or prohibited things becomes the opposite of all this. Beware of eating excessively and frequently eating to satiety, for even if from lawful foods it will still be the beginning of many evils. It results in hardening of the heart, loss of perspicacity, confused thinking, laziness in worship, and other such things. The way to be moderate is to stop eating while still desiring to eat, and not to start eating until you really want food. The sign of that is that you find yourself ready to accept any kind of food at all. When you drink water, sip it, and do not gulp it down. Stop to breathe three times while drinking; do not breathe into the cup, neither drink from where it is cracked, nor standing up, nor from the mouth of the waterskin. If you find no container, drink from your hand. Once you are finished say, "*Al-ḥamdu lil'llāhi'lladhī ja'alahu 'adhban furātan biraḥmatihi wa-lam yaj'alhu milḥan ujājan bidhunūbinā.*" [Praised be God Who made it sweet and limpid through his mercy, and not salty and bitter through our sins.][13]

When you approach your wife sexually say, "*Bismillāh. Allāhumma jannibna'l-shayṭāna, wa jannib il-shayṭāna mā razaqtanā.*" [In the Name of God. O God, keep the Devil away

---

11. This means that one should eat dry food at times and not get habituated to luxury.

12. Bayhaqī, *Shu'ab al-Īmān,*5281; Ibn Abī al-Dunyā, *Kitāb al-Samt*, 150.

13. Bayhaqī, *Shu'ab al-Īmān,*4162; Ṭabarānī, *al-Du'ā'*, 899.

from us and from the [offspring] that You give us!][14] Keep yourself and your wife well covered and behave quietly and serenely. When you feel that orgasm is near, recite within yourself, without moving your lips, His saying, Exalted is He, ***Wa huwa'llahī khalaqa minal-mā'i basharan.***[15] [***He it is who created man out of water.***]

As for whether to marry or not, the best choice for a worshipper will be that which, from the religious point of view, is safer, better for his heart, and more conducive for his mind to remain collected. It is extremely reprehensible for those who are not married to think about women in such a manner as to increase their desire. Anyone thus afflicted, and unable to control it with acts of worship, must get married. If he is unable to, let him fast, for this diminishes desire.

When you enter the lavatory for either of the excretory functions, wear your sandals, cover your head, enter with your left foot and exit with your right. Say before entering, "*Bismillāh. Allāhumma innī a'ūdhu bika min'al-khubuthi wal-khabā'ith.* [In the Name of God. O God, I seek your protection from male and female demons.][16] As you come out say, "*Ghufrānak!*[17] *Al-ḥamdu l'illāhi'lladhī adh-haba 'annī l-adhā wa 'āfānī.*" [I seek your forgiveness! Praised be God who removed harm from me and made me healthy.][18] Do not invoke God there except in your heart and do not take in with you anything on which His Name is written, out of reverence for Him. Do not act frivolously, speak only when strictly necessary, raise your clothes only to the extent of protecting them from getting soiled, keep well away from anybody's sight, and let neither sound nor smell be noticed. Neither face the *Qibla* nor turn your back to it. This may be difficult in some buildings, at which time it becomes allowed not to because of the hardship involved. Never urinate in stagnant water, even if it is a large quantity, except when unavoidable, nor on solid ground, nor

14. Bukhārī, *Ṣaḥīḥ*, 141; Muslim, *Ṣaḥīḥ*, 1434.

15. Qur'ān, 25:54.

16. Bukhārī, *Ṣaḥīḥ*, 142; Muslim, *Ṣaḥīḥ*, 375. Malevolent jinn who are likely to be present in the bathroom and other dirty places

17. Abū Dāwūd, *Sunan*, 30; Tirmidhī, *Sunan*, 7.

18. Nasā'ī, *al-Sunan al-Kubra*, 9825; Ibn Māja, *Sunan*, 301.

against the wind. This is to avoid getting soiled with urine, which results in much of the grave's torment. Therefore, clean yourself from it thoroughly, but without falling into obsessiveness. This is helped by coughing and emptying the penis by massaging its under surface. Clean your anal region with stones, then water. If only one of them is to be used, then water is preferable. Begin with the genital region when using water and the anal region when using stones. Say afterwards, "*Allāhumma ḥaṣṣin farjī mina'l-fawāḥish, wa ṭahhir qalbī minna'l-nifāq.*" [O God! Guard my sexual organs against depravity and purify my heart from hypocrisy!]

Use your right hand in everything except in removing defilement and dirt, [and always put your right foot forward except in] entering dirty places, where you should enter with the left.

When you sneeze, try to muffle it; cover your mouth and say, "*Al-ḥamdu lil'llāhi rabbi l-'ālamīn!*" [Praise be God, Lord of the Worlds!] Spit only to your left or near your left foot.

Shut the waterskin's mouth, cover all vessels, and shut the house's door, especially before going to sleep or going out. Do not go to sleep until you have put out or covered all flames such as lamps, and so forth. If you find a vessel uncovered in the morning or a waterskin open, do not drink from them, but only use the water in things for which defiled water can be used, regardless of it being clean, for its use is dangerous. Shaykh ibn 'Arabī said in the *Futūḥāt* that in every year there is an unknown night in which sickness descends, which finds no uncovered vessel nor open waterskin but that it enters therein. This is why the Messenger of God—may blessings and peace be upon him—advised people to close their waterskins and cover their vessels. If you find nothing to cover a vessel with, put a twig on it, utter the Name of God, and place your trust in Him, for indeed God loves those who trust Him.

Chapter 15

On Conduct in Mosques

You must stay for prolonged periods in the mosques with the intention of *i'tikāf* [withdrawal], for mosques are the houses of God and the places most beloved to Him. He has said, may blessings and peace be upon him and his family, *The mosque is the house of all the God-fearing.*[1] And he has said, may blessings and peace be upon him and his family, *When you see a man frequent the mosques, bear witness that he has faith.*[2] God the Exalted has said, ***He only shall attend God's mosques who believes in God and the Last Day.***[3] And the Prophet—may peace be upon him—included among the seven whom God will shade under His Throne on the day when no shade shall exist save His, *a man whose heart remains attached to the mosque from the moment he leaves it until he returns.*[4] You must, when sitting in the mosque have good manners and respect, and refrain from unnecessary, not to mention prohibited, talk. If you feel like talking about something worldly, go out of the mosque. In the mosque, occupy yourself exclusively with worship, for it was built only for the worship of God. He has said, Exalted is He, ***In houses which God allows to be raised, that therein His Name is remembered and He is glorified morning and evening by men whom neither merchandise nor sale distract from remembering God, establishing the prayer and giving out the* Zakāt*: they fear a day when hearts and eyes shall be overturned. That God may reward them with the best of what they did and increase reward for them of His bounty: God gives freely to whom He will.***[5]

1. Bazzār, *Musnad*, 2546; Bayhaqī, *Shu'ab al-Īmān,* 2689, 10174; Ṭabarānī, *Kabīr*, 6143.
2. Ibn Māja, *Sunan*, 802; Bayhaqī, *Shu'ab al-Īmān,* 2680.
3. Qur'ān, 9:18.
4. Ibn Ḥibbān, *Ṣaḥīḥ*, 7338; Bazzār, *Musnad*, 8182.
5. Qur'ān, 24:36, 37, 38.

When you enter the mosque, do so with your right foot and say, *"Bismillāhi wa'ṣ-ṣalātu wa's salāmu 'alā rasūl'illāh, allāhumma'ghfir li dhanbī wa'ftaḥlī abwāba raḥmatik."* [In the Name of God. May blessings and peace be upon the Messenger of God. O God, forgive me my sins and open for me the gates of your mercy!][6] Do not sit down before you pray two *rak'as.* If for any reason you are unable to pray, say four times, *"Subhāna Allāhi, wal-ḥamdu lil'llāhi, wa-lā ilāha illa'llāhu, wa'llāhu akbar."* When you leave do so with your left foot and say what you did when you entered, but say, "*abwāba faḍlik"* instead of "*abwāba raḥmatik.*" And add, "*A'ūdhu billāhi minal-shayṭāni'r- rajīmi wa junūdih.*" [I seek God's protection against the Repudiate Devil and his legions.] When you hear the Call to Prayer, repeat what the Mu'azzin says, until he says, *"Ḥayya 'alā ṣ-ṣalāh"* [hasten to the prayer] and, "*Ḥayya 'ala'l-falāḥ"* [hasten to success] when you should say, *"Lā ḥawla wa-lā quwwata illā bil'llāh"* [There is neither ability nor strength save by God]. And when he says, "*Aṣṣalātu khayrun mina'n-nawm*" [prayer is better than sleep] say, "*Ṣadaqta wa-barart.*" [You have spoken truthfully and beneficially.] When the Call is finished bless the Prophet - may blessings and peace be upon him - and then say, "*Allāhumma rabba hādhihi' d-da'wati't-tāmmah, wa's-ṣalātil-qā'imati āti Muḥammadan al-wasīlata wa'l-faḍīlata wa-b'ath'hu maqāman maḥmūdan alladhī wa'adtah.*" [O God, Lord of this complete call and imminent prayer, grant Muḥammad the Intercession and superiority, and resurrect him to the Praiseworthy Station, even as You have promised him.][7] Make as much *du'ā'* as you can between the *Adhān* and the *Iqāma*, since he has said, may blessings and peace be upon him and his family, *Prayers between the* Adhān *and the* Iqāma *are never turned down.*[8] Among the prayers which have been handed down for this time is, "*Allāhumma innī as'aluka'l-'āfiyah fi'd-dunyā wa'l-ākhira.*" [O God, I ask You for safety in this world and the next!][9] this prayer is recommended in the *Sunna* for other times as well, so use it often for it is one of the best and most comprehensive of all prayers.

---

6. Tirmidhī, *Sunan*, 314; Ibn Māja, *Sunan*, 771.
7. Bukhārī, *Ṣaḥīḥ*, 614.
8. Abū Dāwūd, *Sunan*, 521; Bayhaqī, *al-Sunan al-Kubra*, 1937.
9. Bukhārī, *al-Adab al-Mufrad*; 698; Ibn Māja, *Sunan*, 3871.

Chapter 16

On the Ritual Prayer

You must pray as soon as the time for each prayer comes. Therefore, you should perform your ablutions and enter the mosque before the Call [*adhān*] for the obligatory prayers. If you do not, you should at least begin to get ready for the prayer immediately upon hearing the Call. He has said, may blessings and peace be upon him and his family, *The superiority of the beginning of the time assigned to each Prayer over its end is like the superiority of the hereafter over this world.*[1] And he has said, may blessings and peace be upon him and his family, *At the beginning of the period is the good pleasure of God, while at its end is His forgiveness.*[2]

Take care always to perform the regular *Sunnas* described in the Law, which are those before and after the obligatory prayers. Beware of missing any of these out of complacency, and if ever you do miss any for any excuse, then perform it as soon as possible. Have reverence and an attentive heart when you pray. Stand up in the best manner, intone the Qur'ān and meditate on it, perfect your bowing, prostrations, and all the other essential acts of the Prayer. Be careful also to observe those *Sunnas* and good manners which are indicated in the Law and avoid anything that may either impair the Prayer or just detract from its perfection. If you conform to this, your Prayer will emerge white, glowing, saying, "May God safeguard you as you have safeguarded me!" Otherwise it will come out black, dark, and say, "May God ruin you as you have ruined me!"[3] He has said, may blessings and peace be upon him and his family, *Only that of which the believer*

1. Daylamī, *Musnad al-Firdaws*, 4353.
2. Tirmidhī, *Sunan*, 172; Dāraquṭnī, *Sunan*, 983.
3. Bayhaqī, *Shu'ab al-Īmān,* 2871; Bazzār, *Musnad*, 2691; Ṭabarānī, *Awsaṭ*, 3095.

is conscious during his Prayer is credited him.[4] Al-Ḥasan al-Baṣrī—may God be pleased with him—has said, "Every Prayer in which the heart is not attentive is nearer to punishment [than it is to reward]." The Devil—may God curse him—is intent on distracting the believer during his Prayer, so that the moment he rises to pray he opens for him many doors into the worldly affairs and reminds him of things which were entirely off his mind before. The Accursed's aim is to distract him from concentrating on God and presence with Him, for if a person misses these he will also miss God's turning toward him, and may even come out of his Prayer burdened with sin. This is why the scholars—may God have mercy on them—recommend for the one about to enter his Prayer to recite *Qul a'ūdhu bi-rabbi'n-nās,*[5] as a protection against the Repudiate Devil. You must not confine yourself to the same *sūras* at the same times, except when indicated in the Law, as, for instance, *Sūra Al-Sajda* [The Prostration] and *Al-Insān* [Man][6] on Friday mornings. You must also take care not to confine yourself to short *sūras* such as *Al-Kāfirūn, Al-Ikhlāṣ, Al-Falaq* [Daybreak] and *Al-Nās* [Mankind][7] If you lead the congregational prayer you should make it brief as is recommended in the *ḥadīth* of Mu'ādh—may God be pleased with him—who once led a Prayer and prolonged it so much that a man went to the Messenger of God—may God's blessings and peace be upon him—and complained. The Prophet said to him, *Are you a worker of sedition, O Mu'ādh? Recite:* Sabbiḥ'isma Rabbika'l-A'lā, Wa'l-shamsi wa-ḍuḥāha and Wa'l-layli idhā yaghshā.[8] He who looks into the books of *ḥadīth* will recognize [the truth of] what we have said. It has been related that the last Prayer that the Messenger of God led—may God's blessings and peace be upon him—was a Sunset Prayer in which he recited *Wa'l-mursalāti 'urfan.* [9]

And God guides whom He will to a straight path.

---

4. Ghazālī, *Iḥyā' 'Ulūm al-Dīn*, 1: 159. The *ḥadīth* is not found in the currently available books of *ḥadīth*.
5. Qur'ān, *Sūra* 114.
6. Qur'ān, *Sūras* 37 and 74.
7. Qur'ān, *Sūras* 113 and 114.
8. Qur'ān, *Sūras* 87: The Most High; 91: The Sun; 92: The Night.
9. Qur'ān, *Sūra* 77.

Chapter 17

On Prayer in Congregation

When you pray behind an *Imām* you must follow him properly, for *The* Imām *was appointed only so that people would be led by him.*[1] Beware of preceding him in performing any of the Prayer's components, or of performing them simultaneously with him; rather, you should follow him step by step. He has said, may blessings and peace be upon him, *The forelock of he who bows and rises before the* Imām *is in the Devil's hand.*[2] Try to reach the first rank and compete for it without offending anyone. Beware of staying back when it is possible to advance, for he has said, may blessings and peace be upon him and his family, *Some people will persist in holding back* (that is, from the first rank) *until God holds them back,*[3] that is, from His favor and mercy. And He has said, may blessings and peace be upon him, *God and his angels bless the foremost rank.*[4] And he used to ask forgiveness for those in the first row thrice, and for those in the second row once only.

Assist in making the ranks even and straight. If you are the *imām,* this becomes doubly incumbent upon you. This is an important thing in the Law, but most people are unaware of it. The Messenger of God, may God's blessings and peace be upon him, was very concerned with this matter and used to do it himself, saying, *You will straighten your ranks or God will cause disagreement to separate your hearts.*[5] He ordered them to close the gaps by saying, *By the One in Whose Hand is my soul, I see the Devil penetrating through the gaps in the ranks just as a small lamb might do.*[6]

---

1. Bukhārī, *Ṣaḥīḥ*, 378; Muslim, *Ṣaḥīḥ*, 411.
2. Bazzār, *Musnad*,9404.
3. Muslim, *Ṣaḥīḥ*, 438; Ibn Māja, *Sunan*, 978.
4. Nasā'ī, *Sunan*, 646; Ibn Māja, *Sunan*, 997.
5. Bukhārī, *Ṣaḥīḥ*, 717; Muslim, *Ṣaḥīḥ*, 436.
6. Abū Dāwūd, *Sunan*, 667; Ibn Khuzayma, *Ṣaḥīḥ*, 1545.

Perform the five Prayers in congregation and persevere in this, for the collective prayer is twenty-seven times better than the individual one, as is stated in a sound *ḥadīth*.[7] Beware of missing the collective prayer for no good reason or for an unacceptable one. If, when you arrive, you find that they have already finished praying, or if you are keeping to your house in order to safeguard your religion, you must find someone to pray with so that you may obtain the reward for the collective prayer and escape the threats handed down against those who abandon it, such as his saying, may blessings and peace be upon him and his family, *Certain people must stop neglecting the collective prayer, or else I shall burn their houses with them inside*.[8] And his saying, may peace be upon him, *He who hears the Call, is healthy and unoccupied, yet does not answer it, there is for him no other acceptable prayer*.[9] And Ibn Mas'ūd—may God be pleased with him—said, "We have seen [a time] when no-one held back [from the collective prayer] except hypocrites whose hypocrisy was obvious." In the days of the Messenger of God—may God's blessings and peace be upon him—they used to bring men [who had to be] supported between two men until they were stood in the rank.[10] This is how severely those who neglect the obligatory collective prayers are regarded.

If there is such a severe insistence on the collective prayer in general, how do you think it is with the Friday Prayer which is an obligation to each individual? The Messenger of God—may God's blessings and peace be upon him—said, *The heart of he who neglects three Friday Prayers because he holds them in light esteem will be sealed by God*.[11] When you feel that you have an excuse not to attend the Friday or any other collective prayer, imagine that, in the place where the Prayer is held, a man will distribute money to all those present. If you then find in yourself the energy and desire to go, then your excuse is unsound. Be ashamed of God that worldly affairs are dearer to you than what He—Ex-

7. Bukhārī, *Ṣaḥīḥ*, 645; Muslim, *Ṣaḥīḥ*, 650.

8. Bukhārī, *Ṣaḥīḥ*, 644; Muslim, *Ṣaḥīḥ*, 651.

9. Bayhaqī, *al-Sunan al-Kubra*, 5588, 5590; Al-Hakim. *Mustadrak*, 899.

10. Muslim, *Ṣaḥīḥ*, 654.

11. Abū Dāwūd, *Sunan*, 1052; Nasā'ī, *Sunan*, 1369. A heart is 'sealed' when it becomes impervious to the penetration of spiritual light.

alted is He—has in store for you.

And know that an honest excuse will do no more than prevent you from being called to account, while the reward can only be obtained by actually performing the deed. However, the reward can be accorded to some who find it totally impossible to attend, as for instance someone with continuous diarrhea, or who is forcibly prevented from going. It can also be given to some who, although not finding it totally impossible to go, would by attending cause undue hardship to another Muslim. An example of this is the one nursing a very sick person. People with such excuses, provided they feel sad and aggrieved for losing the Prayer, will receive the reward. A perfect believer never abandons any act that would draw him nearer to God, even though he may have a million excuses, unless he knows that not acting is more pleasing to God, and this is very rare. Thus do the perfect among men of God, in doing what takes them nearer to Him, endure that which firmly set mountains cannot endure. As for those whose faith and certainty are weak, and knowledge of God inadequate, when faced with having to miss an obligatory act, they are concerned only with avoiding reproach. ***For each of them will be degrees from what they do, that He may pay them for their deeds, and they will not be wronged.*** [12]

You should charge all those for whom you are responsible, whether child, wife, or slave, with performing the obligatory prayers. Should any of them refuse, you should admonish and put fear into him. Should he rebel and persist in refusing, you may reprimand and physically chastise him; if still he is not rebuked and continues to refuse, then turn away and cease to have anything to do with him. For he who abandons the Prayer is a devil, remote from God's mercy, exposed to his wrath and curses, and all Muslims are prohibited from befriending him and obliged to oppose him. This must be so, for the Messenger of God—may God's blessings and peace be upon him—has said, *The bond that is between us is the Prayer; he who abandons it has disbelieved.*[13] And he has said, may blessings and peace be upon him and his family, *He who does not pray has no religion. The Prayer is to*

12. Qur'ān, 46:19.
13. Tirmidhī, *Sunan*, 2621; Nasā'ī, *Sunan*, 463.

religion what the head is to the body.[14]

Free yourself every Friday from all worldly preoccupations and devote this noble day entirely to the hereafter. Occupy yourself with nothing but goodness and resolute approach to God. Watch carefully for the hour in which requests are granted, which is a period of time in each Friday when any Muslim who asks God for any good or protection from any evil is granted his request.

Be early to the Friday Prayer; get there before the sun reaches its zenith, sit near the pulpit and listen carefully to the sermon; beware of distracting yourself with invocation or reflection, not to mention trivial talk or aimless thoughts. Feel that all the admonition and counseling that you hear is addressed to you personally. Before you move your legs or talk [after the end of the prayer] recite the *Fātiḥa*, *Sūra al-Ikhlāṣ*, *Qul a'ūdhu bi-rabbi'l-falaq* and *Qul a'ūdhu bi-rabbi'n-nās*, seven times each, and say when you leave the Prayer, *Subḥān Allāhi wa-bi-ḥamdih* one hundred times, for there are *ḥadīths* which indicate the merit of this act.[15]

And success is by God.

---

14. Ṭabarānī, *Ṣaghīr*, 152; *Awsaṭ*, 2292.

15. *He who says in a day*: Subḥān Allāhi wa-bi-ḥamdih *one hundred times shall be unburdened of his sins, even were they as the foam of the sea.* [Bukhārī, *Ṣaḥīḥ*, 6405; Muslim, *Ṣaḥīḥ*, 2691.] *He who says morning and evening*, Subḥān Allāhi wa-bi-ḥamdih *one hundred times, none shall come on Resurrection Day having done better, save one who said the same or more.* [Muslim, *Ṣaḥīḥ*, 2692.]

Chapter 18

On Zakāt

When you have money on which *Zakāt* is payable, be aware of when it falls due, define its quantity, separate it from the rest, give it willingly, and intend it to be solely for the sake of God. If you do this, it will attract *baraka*, the good things in your possession will multiply, and your wealth will become well-guarded against all hazards.

You must separate *Zakāt* [from your wealth] before distributing it. Do not be like certain worldly people who do not keep it separate and give it away piecemeal to deserving people as they come along, until the amount to be spent is all paid. Do not eat of your crops once they amount to a *niṣāb*[1] and they are seen to be healthy until you know how much of their dry weight will be due. If you want to eat from certain specific trees, then you can calculate only that which will be due from them.[2]

Know that those who devise ruses to escape giving *Zakāt*—for instance those who give gifts,[3] those who knowingly give it to people who do not deserve it, and those who distribute it according to their whims, as for instance by giving it to someone whom they know will soon be useful to them—none of these shall leave the world until God has punished them through their wealth, ***and the torment of the hereafter is even greater, if they but knew.***[4] And if this is the state of those who do not give it away strictly according to the Law, what must it be in the case of those who do not give it at all? ***Those are they who purchase error at the price***

1. *Niṣāb* is the minimum number of possessions necessary for *Zakāt* to become due.

2. In order to permit oneself to consume of the produce of certain specific trees, one should calculate the amount of *Zakāt* to be paid for those, in isolation from the rest of the trees.

3. These are people who give away gifts to reduce their possessions below the minimum level at which *Zakāt* becomes due.

4. Qur'ān, 58:33.

of guidance, so their commerce does not prosper, neither are they guided.[5]

The withholder of *Zakāt* is as evil as the one who leaves the ritual prayer. Abū Bakr—may God be pleased with him—fought them and called them apostates [*murtaddūn*].

You must give *Zakāt al-Fiṭr* [at the end of Ramaḍān] if you have enough to, for yourself and on behalf of all those for whom you provide.

Be liberal with charity, especially to needy relatives and poor people of virtue. Charity is better and brings more reward when given in this way. Give of that which you like best and which is dear to you so that you may attain to virtue. God the Exalted has said, ***You will not attain to virtue until you spend of that which you love.***[6] Put others before yourself even in times of need and you will become one of the successful. Keep your charity secret, for secret charity extinguishes the Lord's wrath, is seventy times better than public charity, and is safe from the ostentation that ruins deeds.

Never neglect to give something away every day, even if a small amount, and do this early, for hardships do not cross [the protective barrier of] charity. Never disappoint a beggar who stands at your door; give him even as little as a date or less, for he is a gift from God to you. If you find nothing to give, then send him away graciously with kind words and a promise.

When you give a needy person something, smile at him affably and bring to your mind that it is you who are indebted to him, for he accepts a little from you for which you receive a reward worth more than the whole world. It has been said that a single morsel of food may bring a reward from God greater than Mount Uḥud.

Do not let the fear of poverty prevent you from giving charity, for it is the abandonment of charity which brings on poverty. Charity on the contrary attracts wealth. If the pursuer of the world gave much charity it would return to him multiplied. Know that charity has immediate and long-term benefits; in the immediate term, it increases provision, lengthens life, protects from an evil

5. Qur'ān, 2:16.
6. Qur'ān, 3:92.

death, gives bodily health, and puts *baraka* into wealth. Later on, it will extinguish sins as water extinguishes fire, shade the head of its giver on Resurrection Day, protect him from punishment, and many other things. ***Only those who repent remember***.[7]

7. Qur'ān, 40:13.

Chapter 19

On Fasting

Increase your good works, especially in Ramaḍān, for the reward of a supererogatory act performed during it equals that of an obligatory act performed at any other time. Ramaḍān is also a time when good works are rendered easy and one has much more energy for them than during any other month. This is because the soul, lazy when it comes to good works, is then imprisoned by hunger and thirst, the devils who hinder it are shackled, the gates of the Fire are shut, the gates of the Garden are open, and the herald calls every night at God's command, "O you who wish for goodness, hasten! O you who wish for evil, halt!"[1]

You should work solely for the hereafter in this noble month, only embarking on something worldly when absolutely necessary. Organize your life before Ramaḍān in such a manner as to render you free for worship once it is here. Be intent on devotions and approach God more surely, especially during the last ten days. If you are able not to leave the mosque, except when strictly necessary, during those last ten days, then do so. Be careful to perform the *Tarāwīḥ* Prayers during every Ramaḍān night. In some places nowadays it has become the custom to make them so short that sometimes some of the obligatory elements of the prayer are omitted, let alone the *Sunnas*. It is well known that our predecessors recited the whole Qur'ān during this prayer, reciting a part each night so as to complete it on one of the last nights of the month. If you are able to follow suit, then this will be a great gain; if not, then the least that you can do is to observe the obligatory elements of the Prayer and its proprieties.

Watch carefully for the Night of Destiny [*Laylat'ul-Qadr*], which is ***better than thousand months***.[2] It is the ***blessed night in***

1. Nasā'ī, *Sunan*, 2107; Aḥmad, *Musnad*, 23491.
2. Qur'ān, 95:11.

which all affairs are wisely decided.[3] He to whom it is unveiled sees the blazing lights, the open doors of heaven, and the angels ascending and descending, and may witness the whole of creation prostrating before God, its Creator.

Most scholars are of the opinion that it is in the last ten nights of Ramaḍān, and is more likely to fall in the odd numbered ones. A certain Knower witnessed it on the night of the seventeenth, and this was also the opinion of al-Ḥasan al-Baṣrī. Some scholars have said that it is the first night of Ramaḍān, and a number of great scholars have said that it is not fixed but shifts its position each Ramaḍān. They have said that the secret wisdom underlying this is that the believer should devote himself completely to God during every night of this month in the hope of coinciding with that night which has been kept obscure from him; and God knows best.

Hasten to break your fast as soon as you are certain that the sun has set. Delay *suḥūr*[4] so long as you do not fear the break of dawn. Feed those who fast at the time when they break it, even if with some dates or a draught of water, for the one who feeds another at the time of breaking the fast receives as much reward as he without this diminishing the other's reward in any way. Be careful never to break your fast, nor to feed anyone else at such a time, except with lawful food. Do not eat much, take whatever lawful food is present, and do not prefer that which is tasty, for the purpose of fasting is to subdue one's lustful appetite, and eating a large quantity of delicious food will on the contrary arouse and strengthen it.

Fast on the days on which the Law encourages you to fast, such as the Day of 'Arafāt for those who are not participating in the pilgrimage, the ninth and tenth days ['Āshūrā'[5]] of Muḥarram and the six days of Shawwāl, starting with the second day of the

3. Qur'ān, 44:4.

4. Suḥūr is the pre-dawn meal.

5. 'Āshūrā' is the tenth day of the month of Muḥarram, the day Moses—may peace be upon him—and his people fled from Pharaoh and his army. When the Prophet, may God's blessings and peace be upon him, on arrival at Madina, found the Jews fasting that day, he said that he and his followers were closer to Moses than the Madina Jews and had therefore more justification to fast that day. Years later it also became a day of grief, the day when the Prophet's grandson Imām Ḥusayn and his family were slain on the field of Karbalā'.

Feast, for this is effective discipline for the soul. Fast three days in each month, for these equal a perpetual fast.[6] It is better if these are the White Days,[7] for the Prophet—may God's blessings and peace be upon him—never omitted to fast them whether he was at home or traveling. Fast often, especially in times of special merit such as the Sacred Months,[8] and noble days such as Mondays and Thursdays.[9]

Know that fasting is the pillar of discipline and the basis of striving. It has been said that fasting constitutes half of fortitude. The Messenger of God—may God's blessings and peace be upon him—said, *God the Exalted has said, "All good deeds of the son of Adam are multiplied ten to seven hundredfold, except fasting, for it is mine, and I shall reward a man for it, for he has left his appetite and his food and drink for my sake!" The one who fasts has two joys, one when breaking his fast, the other when meeting his Lord; and the odor of the fasting man's mouth is more fragrant to God than that of musk.*[10]

God says the truth and He guides to the way.[11]

6. The reward for a good deed being ten times its value, a three-days fast will bring a reward equal to thirty days, which is equivalent to fasting every single day of the month.

7. The nights when the moon is at its fullest, which are the 13th, 14th, and 15th of each lunar month.

8. Dhū al-Qa'da, Dhū al-Ḥajja, and Muḥarram: the three months of the Ḥajj season. The fourth is Rajab. They were held sacred because the Arabs had agreed to stop raiding and fighting in them to allow the pilgrims to reach Makka, perform the Pilgrimage, and return home safely.

9. Mondays and Thursdays are the days when people's deeds are reported to God, the doors of Heaven are opened, and forgiveness is swift. The Prophet was born on a Monday; he received the first Qur'ānic revelations on a Monday, and died in Madina on a Monday.

10. Bukhārī, *Ṣaḥīḥ*, 1904; Muslim, *Ṣaḥīḥ*, 1151.

11. Qur'ān, 33:4.

Chapter 20

On Pilgrimage

Hasten to perform the obligations of Ḥajj and *'Umra* as soon as you are able. Beware of postponing them while able, for you may lose the ability, or die while this duty is still incumbent, and you will then be deemed neglectful. The Prophet has said, may God's blessings and peace be upon him and his family, *He who is not prevented by manifest necessity, disabling sickness, or a tyrannical ruler, and dies having not performed the Ḥajj, let him die a Jew if he so chooses, or a Christian if he so chooses.*[1]

Also, whenever able, perform supererogatory acts of Ḥajj and *'Umra*, just as you perform any other supererogatory devotion. It has been handed down that *God the Exalted has said, "Any servant whose body I have made healthy and whose wealth I have made abundant, and who lets five years go by without coming to Me, is indeed deprived."*[2]

When you decide to go on Ḥajj, you must learn its obligatory acts, its *Sunnas*, and its invocations. You must also learn how to locate the *Qibla*, the concessions allowed during travelling and other associated proprieties, and the invocations to be said.

Do not intend both Ḥajj and commerce at the same time. You should only take such worldly goods as you intend to spend on the road. If you must, then avoid anything that may distract you from the correct performance and due respect for the rites ordained by God.

You must visit the Messenger of God—may God's blessings and peace be upon him—for visiting him after his death is like visiting him during his life. He is alive in his grave, as are all the other Prophets. It is churlish to go to the House of God for Ḥajj and then neglect to visit God's Beloved for no overwhelming reason. Know that if you had come [walking] on your head from the

---

1. Dārimī, *Sunan*, 1826; Bayhaqī, *Shu'ab al-Īmān* 3693; Abū Ya'lā, *Musnad*, 231.

2. *Ḥadīth Qudsī,* Ibn Ḥibbān, *Ṣaḥīḥ*, 3703; Bayhaqī, *Shu'ab al-Īmān* 3838.

farthest land of Islam to visit him—may blessings and peace be upon him—you would not even have begun to render thanks for the guidance that God gave you through him.

When you wish to do something of consequence such as traveling or marrying, consult one of your brothers in whose knowledge and experience you are confident. If the advice he gives you conforms to what you have in mind, then pray two supererogatory *rak'as* with the intention of making the right choice [*Istikhāra*] and say afterwards the well-known prayer. The Prophet has said, may blessings and peace be upon him and his family, *He who does* Istikhāra *never fails, and he who consults never regrets it.*[3]

If you ever make a vow [*nadhr*] to God, whether it takes the form of prayers, charity, or anything else, hasten to fulfill it. Do not get used to making frequent vows, for Satan may lure you into this to induce you to default.

If you swear to do something, and then find it better not to do it, or *vice versa*, take the course you think is best, then expiate for your oath. Beware of swearing or testifying on the basis of conjecture, even if you are almost certain, let alone when it is illusory or dubious. If your oath ever leads you to take another Muslim's money [wrongly], your duty is to return what you have taken and expiate for your oath. This consists in either feeding ten indigent people with a measure of food [*mudd*] each, or clothing them, or setting free a slave. If you can do none of these, then fast for three days.

Never swear falsely, for this destroys homes and plunges the one who does it in the fire of Hell.

Beware greatly of false testimony, for it is one of the greatest sins, and the Prophet—may God's blessings and peace be upon him—has associated it with idolatry. If to abstain from testifying [when able to] is a great sin, what then must be the case with deliberate falsification? We ask God for safety before the advent of regret.

3. Ṭabarānī, *Ṣaghīr*, 980; *Awsaṭ*, 6627; Al-Shihāb, *Musnad*, 774.

Chapter 21

On Scrupulousness

You must scrupulously avoid both prohibited and suspect things. Scrupulousness or circumspection [*wara'*] is the pillar and pivot of religion and its importance is always emphasized by those scholars who practice what they know. The Messenger of God—may God's blessings and peace be upon him—said, *All flesh that has grown on wrongfully acquired money, the Fire has first right to it.*[1] And he said, may blessings and peace be upon him and his family, *He who guards himself against suspect things protects his religion and his honor, while he who falls into suspect things will eventually fall into the prohibited.*[2]

Know that those who acquire prohibited and suspect things are seldom granted success in performing good deeds, and when they appear to be doing so, these are inevitably inwardly tarnished with hidden flaws which spoil them, such as conceit and ostentation. The works of those who subsist on unlawful resources are always rejected, for God is good and accepts only that which is good. The explanation for this is that one can only act using one's bodily members, which can only move by the energy obtained from food. If that food is vile, the energy it produces and the movements which result will also be vile. 'Abd Allāh ibn 'Umar,[3] may God be pleased with him and his father, has said, "Were you to pray until your backs become bent and fast until you become [thin] like strings, God will only accept if it is done with safeguarding scrupulousness." And it has been reported that the Messenger of God—may God's blessings and peace be upon him—has said,

1. Dārimī, *Sunan*, 2818; Bayhaqī, *Shu'ab al-Īmān* 5375; Aḥmad, *Musnad*, 14441.

2. Muslim, *Ṣaḥīḥ*, 1599; Ibn Māja, *Sunan*, 3984.

3. 'Abd Allāh, son of the second Caliph, 'Umar ibn al-Khaṭṭāb, was one of the most pious and knowledgeable Companions, and one of the few who have transmitted over one thousand *ḥadīths* each.

The prayers of a man who buys a garment for ten Dirhams, one of which is unlawful, will not be accepted by God as long as he is wearing any part of it.[4] If this is how it is with a garment for which one-tenth of the price is unlawful, what if the whole of it was so? And if this is how it is with garments worn on the outside of the body, what about nutrition that runs through the veins and joints and infiltrates the whole body?

Know that prohibited things are of two categories: the first is what is prohibited in itself, as for instance carrion, blood, and alcohol. These can never become permissible except in dire necessity when they are the only things available and one's very survival depends on them. The second is that which is lawful in itself, such as wheat and clean water, but owned by someone else, thus remaining unlawful until acquired by lawful means such as buying or receiving as a gift or an inheritance.

As for doubtful or suspect things, they are of many degrees. Some you may be convinced of their being prohibited but still entertain the possibility of their being lawful; these should be considered prohibited. Others you may be convinced are lawful, but a suspicion exists that they may be prohibited; these should be avoided out of scrupulousness. Other things lie between these two degrees, for instance things which have an equal chance of being lawful or unlawful. The Prophet has said, may God's blessings and peace be upon him and his family, *Leave what which arouses your suspicion for that which does not.*[5] A man's scrupulousness is measured by his abstaining from anything suspect until its status is clarified. A servant [of God] does not become a truly God-fearing man until he abstains from things which are undoubtedly lawful for fear of that which may follow and be doubtful or unlawful. The Prophet has said, may God's blessings and peace be upon him and his family, *A servant does not attain the rank of the God-fearing until he abstains from that which is harmless for fear of [falling into] that which is harmful.*[6] And the Companions—may God be pleased with them—used to say, "We used to leave seventy lawful avenues for fear of falling into the unlawful." But

4. Aḥmad, *Musnad*, 5732; Bayhaqī, *Shu'ab al- Īmān*, 5707.
5. Tirmidhī, *Sunan*, 2518; Nasā'ī, *Sunan*, 5711.
6. Tirmidhī, *Sunan*, 2451; Ibn Māja, *Sunan*, 4215.

this is something that has long gone. Where are we now to find such scrupulousness as will keep us from suspect and unlawful things? Ability and strength are only by God.

You must know everything that God has forbidden so as to be able to avoid it, for he who cannot recognize evil falls into it.

Know that a religious man is not likely to do anything which is unlawful in itself, such as eating forbidden animals or wrongfully appropriating other people's money by coercion, injustice, theft, or pillage, for these usually proceed from hard oppressive men and rebellious demons.[7] Religious people, however, remain prey to ambiguities because they neglect three things:

Firstly, they do not investigate thoroughly where this is appropriate. To explain: In your dealings with people, you should see them as falling into one of three categories:

- The first comprises those whom you know to be good and virtuous. You may eat their food and transact with them without further inquiry.
- The second comprises those you know nothing about, whether good or bad. When you wish to transact with them or accept their gifts, then scrupulousness obliges you to inquire, but tactfully. Should you feel that this may offend them, then silence is better.
- The third comprises those you know to be wrongdoers, usurers for instance, or people careless about their buying and selling and not really concerned where the money comes from. It is better not to transact with such people at all, but if you must, then investigate and inquire beforehand, as scrupulousness demands, until you know which of their lawful possessions are free from suspicion, and then still be careful. If any object reaches you that you know from appearances or suspect to be unlawful, then do not hesitate to refuse it, even if given to you by the most virtuous of men.

Secondly, they do not safeguard themselves against invalid and discouraged transactions. Therefore, neither sell nor buy from them except by valid contract. There is no harm, however, in trans-

7. Demons can be men or jinn, the term being used to designate a particularly evil kind of behavior rather than any particular kind of creature.

actions without contract if involving only insignificant things.

Avoid cheating, lying, and making oaths concerning merchandise. Do not hide a defect in your merchandise which, if seen by the buyer, would prevent him from paying the same price.

Beware greatly of usury, for it is one of the worst major sins. God the Exalted says, ***O believers, fear God and renounce whatever usury is still owed to you, if you are [truly] believers. If you do not, then be warned of war from God and His Messenger.***[8] And the Messenger of God—may God's blessings and peace be upon him—has cursed the taker of usury, his client, clerk, and witness.[9] The summation of [the law for] usury is that it is unlawful to trade money for its kind, for instance silver for silver, and food for its kind, for instance wheat for wheat, except when the amounts exchanged are exactly equal. If the kinds differ, for example gold for silver, or dates for wheat, differences in value are allowed and payment should be immediate. There is no usury in trading an animal for an animal, a garment for a garment, or food for money.

Beware of monopoly (*iḥtikār*), which is to buy food which is much needed, and then hoard it until the price goes up.

Thirdly, they are engrossed in the world's cravings and excessively indulge in its pleasures. Scrupulousness under such circumstances becomes difficult and the lawful is narrowed down, for this is extravagance, and the lawful do not bear extravagance.

On the other hand, scrupulousness is rendered easy for those who desire only what is necessary from the world. The Proof of Islam—may God spread his benefit—has said, "If you are content with one rough robe a year and two loaves of coarse grain every day, you will never be short of your lawful sufficiency, for the lawful is abundant. You are not required to investigate deep into everything, but just to be wary of that which you either know is unlawful or suspect it to be so from clear signs indicating the status of the money."

When your suspicions are aroused, then circumspection obliges you to abstain, even though that thing may be, to all out-

8. Qur'ān, 2: 278, 279.

9. Abū Dāwūd, *Sunan*, 3333; Tirmidhī, *Sunan*, 1206; Ibn Māja, *Sunan*, 2277.

ward appearances, lawful. For sin is that which arouses inward suspicion and hesitation, even should you be given a legal opinion by those entitled to give them, as the Prophet stated—may God's blessings and peace be upon him.[1] But this concerns those whose hearts are illuminated and who incline toward abstinence, rather than indulgence.

Do not think that scrupulousness involves only food and clothes; rather, it involves everything. However, if you have in your possession both lawful and more purely lawful, or lawful and suspect things, then use the most lawful that you have in matters of nutrition. Everything depends on food, for when it is lawful it has a great illuminating influence on the heart and provides the body with energy for worship. One of our predecessors has said, "Eat what you will, for in the same wise your actions will be." And Ibrāhīm ibn Adham—may God have mercy on him—has said, "Eat good food and you will no longer need to pray by night, or fast by day."[2]

Know this! God it is who grants success.

1. Aḥmad, *Musnad*, 18001; Dārimī, *Sunan*, 1586.

2. Ibrāhīm ibn Adham is one of the great Sufis of the earliest generation. His utterance stresses the importance of eating nothing but entirely lawful, free-of-suspicion food, but does not mean that night vigils and day fasts are unnecessary.

Chapter 22

On Enjoining Good and Forbidding Evil

You must enjoin good and forbid evil, for this is the pivot around which religion revolves, and the reason why God revealed His Books and sent His Messengers. It is considered a duty by Muslim consensus. A great many passages in the Book and *Sunna* enjoin it and warn about its neglect. God the Exalted says, ***Let there be from among you a community who invite to goodness, enjoin good, and forbid evil. Such are they who are successful.***[3] In many contexts has God attributed enjoining good and forbidding evil to the believers, on some occasions [even] before attributing faith to them, or before mentioning the regular performance of ritual prayers and the paying of *Zakāt*. He says, Exalted is He, ***Those of the children of Israel who disbelieved were cursed by the tongue of David and Jesus, son of Mary, because they rebelled and used to transgress. They forbade not one another the wickedness they did. Indeed, evil was what they used to do.***[4] And He says, Exalted is He, ***And guard yourselves against a chastisement which shall not exclusively fall on those of you who do wrong.***[5] The Messenger of God—may God's blessings and peace be upon him—has said, *Anyone of you who sees a reprehensible thing should change it with his hands; if unable to, then with his tongue, and if still unable to, then with his heart, which thing is the weakest degree of faith.*[6] And he has said, may God's blessings and peace be upon him and his family, *By the One in whose hand lies my soul, you will enjoin good and forbid evil, or God will soon send His punishment upon you, whereupon you will*

3. Qur'ān, 3:104.
4. Qur'ān, 5:78, 79.
5. Qur'ān, 8:25.
6. Muslim, *Ṣaḥīḥ*, 78; Abū Dāwūd, *Sunan*, 1140; Nasā'ī, *Sunan*, 5008.

pray and not be answered.[7] And he has said, may blessings and peace be upon him, *He is not one of us who is not compassionate to our young and respectful to our elders, and who does not enjoin good and forbid evil.*[8]

Know that enjoining good and forbidding evil is a collective obligation [*farḍ kifāya*], which if discharged by some, the rest are relieved from its burden, the reward being proper to those who discharge it. If no one does it, then everyone who is aware of it and able to act is held responsible. Your duty, when you see someone neglecting an act of goodness or committing an act of evil, is to make him aware of the good or evil nature of the act, as the case may be. If he does not respond, you must counsel and put fear into him; if he is still not rebuked, then you must coerce him and [even] beat and compel him [to stop the evil he is engaged in], and break the forbidden instruments of distraction, pour away the wine, and restore unlawful money to its rightful owner. This last degree, however, is only for those who have either dedicated themselves wholly to God or are authorized delegates of the ruler. Those who neglect the first two degrees, which are the appraisal [of things as good and evil] and counselling, are either confused ignorant people or inadequate scholars.

Know that to enjoin good and forbid prohibited things are obligations, while to enjoin recommended and forbid discouraged things are recommended activities.

Whenever you enjoin good or forbid evil and are not listened to, you must leave the place where evil is being committed and those who commit it until such time as they return to God's ordinance. You must also detest sins and those who persistently commit them, and abhor them for the sake of God, this being a duty to all believers.

When you are wronged or insulted and become angry and it shows on your face, and you find that your loathing of that deed and the person who did it are more than your loathing of any other evil you see or hear about, then know for certain that your faith is weak, and that your honor and wealth are dearer to you than your religion.

---

7. Tirmidhī, *Sunan*, 2169; Bayhaqī, *Shu'ab al-Īmān*, 7152; Aḥmad, *Musnad*, 23301.

8. Tirmidhī, *Sunan*, 1921.

You are permitted to remain silent if you know for certain that if you do enjoin good or forbid evil you will neither be listened to, nor will your words be accepted, or that there will ensue obvious harm to yourself or your property. This is when the status of enjoining and forbidding changes from being an obligation into being a tremendous virtue that indicates that he who practices it loves God and prefers Him to all else. But if you come to know that an evil will increase if forbidden, or that the harm will involve Muslims other than yourself, then silence is better and in certain cases obligatory.

Beware of dissimulation, for it is a crime. This is to remain silent for fear of losing your position, money, or any other benefit, the source of which is either the person committing the reprehensible act or any other corrupt person.

Know that whenever you enjoin or forbid something it should be done sincerely for God, Exalted is He, tactfully, wisely, and with compassion, for these attributes never combine in a person who both acts and refrains from acting in accordance with His injunctions but that his words become effective and evoke reverence, a powerful response from the heart, and a sweetness in the ears; seldom shall his words be rejected.

He who has true vigilance for God and reliance upon Him, and has acquired the attribute of mercy towards God's servants, cannot prevent himself from removing every evil that he sees, except when prevented by means he cannot overcome.

Beware of spying, which is seeking to know the private affairs of other Muslims and their hidden sins. The Prophet has said, may God's blessings and peace be upon him and his family, *He who seeks out the secrets of his brother Muslim, God shall seek out his secrets until He exposes him, even to the depths of his own house.*[9]

Know that a concealed sin harms only its doer; but once it becomes public and is left unchecked, its harm becomes general.

When sins and reprehensible things become obscenely in evidence where you live, and you despair of truth being accepted, then isolate yourself, for in this lies safety; or emigrate to another place, which is even better. For when chastisement befalls a place,

9. Tirmidhī, *Sunan*, 2032; Bayhaqī, *Shu'ab al-Īmān,* 10682.

it includes both the wicked and the good. To the believer who was neglectful in supporting God's religion, it is expiation and a mercy, but for others it is a chastisement and an affliction. And God knows best.

Chapter 23
On Social Duties

Deal justly with those in your charge, whether 'personal' or 'public'. Be altogether protective and solicitous for them, for God—Exalted is He—will call you to account in their regard, *and every shepherd will be asked to account for his flock.*[1]

By 'personal charges' I mean your seven organs, which are your tongue, ears, eyes, stomach, genitals, hands, and feet. These are your charges which God has given you and a trust with which He has entrusted you, and you should restrain them from sin and use them in His obedience. For God the Exalted created them only that by means of them you might obey Him; they are among the greatest of His favors, for which you should thank Him—Transcendent is He—by using them to obey Him, and not in His disobedience. If you do not do this, you will be turning God's favor into ingratitude. Had God the Exalted not made these organs to be your servants and made them to obey you by disposition, you would never have been able to use them to disobey Him. When you intend to use any of them sinfully, it says in its own way, "O servant of God, fear God! Do not force me to commit that which God has forbidden me!" If you then do commit the sin, it turns to God and says, "I forbade him, O Lord, but he did not listen; I am innocent of what he did." You will one day stand before God the Exalted and these organs will testify for you to every good and against you to every evil in which you used them, on ***a day which cannot be averted, brought on by God, you will then have neither refuge nor denial,***[2] ***a day when wealth and children will avail nothing, save those who come to God with a whole heart.***[3]

1. Bukhārī, *Ṣaḥīḥ*, 893; Muslim, *Ṣaḥīḥ*, 1829.

2. Qur'ān, 42:47. This is when there will be no possibility of either hiding or denying the evil one is charged with committing.

3. Qur'ān, 26:89. A 'whole heart' is one which is pure of evil thoughts, feelings, and images, and in the context of Prophets and saints, one which is

As for your 'public charges,' these are the people entrusted by God to your custody, such as child, wife, and slave, all of whom are part of your charge. It is your duty to guide them to the performance of that which God has made obligatory and the avoidance of that which He forbade. Beware of allowing them to neglect an obligatory or commit a forbidden act. Invite them to that where their salvation and happiness in the hereafter lies. Teach them courtesy and do not plant in their hearts the love of the world and its cravings, for you would thus have done them harm. It has been said that the wife and children of a man shall clutch at him before God and say, "O Lord, he did not teach us Your rights upon us; therefore, give us requital from him!"

You must treat them with justice and graciousness. Justice is to give them everything that God has made rightfully theirs in the way of expenditure, clothes, and treating them with benevolence. One of its obligations is to prevent them from wronging each other and take the wronged one's rights from the unjust among them. A *ḥadīth* says, *A man may be written down a tyrant when he has power only over his family,*[4] that is, when he treats them high-handedly.

As for graciousness, this is to treat them gently, not to be harsh in asking them for the rights assigned to you by God, treat them with nobility, and laugh with them at times, without falling into sin, in a manner that removes estrangement and repugnance, but maintains reverence and respect.

You should forgive the wrongdoers among them and those who offend you. Secretly absolve them for what they may have embezzled of your wealth, for this will eventually be added to your good deeds, and it is not fitting that they should be punished because of you, while you are rewarded because of them. The Messenger of God—may God's blessings and peace be upon him—was once asked, "How many times should a slave be forgiven each day?" and he replied, *Seventy times.*[5] This forgiveness concerns your rights upon them, but never those of God.

---

unblemished by the least regard for anything other than God.

4. Abū Nu'aym, *Ḥilyat al-Awliyā'*, 8/289; Ibn Ḥajar al-'Asqalānī, *al-Maṭālib al-'Āliya,* 2577; Ṭabarānī, *Awsaṭ,* 6273.

5. Aḥmad, *Musnad,* 8047.

Devote special protection and solicitude to the women of your household, for they are wanting in reason and religion. Teach them the rules pertaining to menstruation, the obligations of *ghusl, wuḍū'*, praying, fasting, the rights of the husband, and other similar things.

Responsibility may be extensive and involve many people, as in the case with rulers and scholars. *Each shepherd will be asked to account for his flock.*[6] God the Exalted says, ***God enjoins justice and goodness.***[7] And he has said, may God's blessings and peace be upon him and his family, *O God, treat gently those who are given authority over any of my community and treat them gently, and treat harshly those who treat them harshly.*[8] And he has said, may blessings and peace be upon him and his family, *No ruler dies having cheated his subjects but that God forbids the Garden to him.*[9]

Be loyal to your parents, for this is a most certain duty. Beware of offending them, for this is one of the greatest major sins. God the Exalted says, ***Your Lord has decreed that you worship none other than Him and treat your parents excellently. If one or both of them attain old age with you, say not "Fie!" to them, nor rebuke them, but speak gracious words to them. And, out of mercy, lower to them the wing of humility, and say, 'My Lord, have mercy on them as they did care for me when I was little.'***[10] And He says, Exalted is He, ***Give thanks to Me and your two parents.***[11] Notice how He associates the exhortation to treat them well with the unification of Him, and thanking them with thanking Him.

You must, therefore, seek to make them pleased with you, and obey them except in committing sinful things or omitting obligations. Give them preference over yourself and their affairs priority over yours.

Disloyalty includes harming them by withholding any good

6. Bukhārī, *Ṣaḥīḥ*, 2409; Muslim, *Ṣaḥīḥ*, 144.
7. Qur'ān, 16:90.
8. Ibn Ḥibbān, *Ṣaḥīḥ*, 553; Aḥmad, *Musnad*, 26199.
9. Bukhārī, *Ṣaḥīḥ*, 7151; Muslim, *Ṣaḥīḥ*, 142.
10. Qur'ān, 17:23, 24.
11. Qur'ān, 31:14.

that you are able to bring them, as well as frowning and chiding. He has said, may God's blessings and peace be upon him, *The scent of the Garden is perceived at a thousand years' distance, but not by he who is disloyal* [*to his parents*], *who severs his kinship bonds, the adulterous old man, or he who lengthens his garment out of vanity, for pride is solely the attribute of God, the Lord of the Worlds.*[12] And he has said, may God's blessings and peace be upon him, that God the Exalted says, *The one upon whom morning comes and he has done what pleases his parents but displeases Me, I am pleased with him; but he upon whom morning comes and he has done what displeases his parents but pleases Me, I am displeased with him.*

Parents should help their children to be loyal to them by not insisting on every single right of theirs, especially these days when loyalty is scarce, evil rife, and parents consider the most loyal of their children to be the one who does not injure them. The Messenger of God—may God's blessings and peace be upon him—has said, *May God have mercy on a parent who helps his child be loyal to him.*[13]

Respect your ties of kinship and start with the closest to you; give generously of the good things you have and start with the nearest. God the exalted says, ***Worship God, associate nothing with Him, behave with excellence toward parents, near kindred, orphans, the indigent, the neighbor who is of kin, and the neighbor who is not.***[14]

God enjoins kindness toward kin in many passages in His August Book; and the Messenger of God—may God's blessings and peace be upon him—has said, *Charity to kin is both charity and preservation* [of kinship bonds].[15] And, *Let him who believes in God and the Last Day preserve his kinship ties.*[16] And, *Let him who believes in God and the Last Day honor his neighbor.*[17] And, *Gabriel has so recommended the neighbor to me that I thought he*

12. Ṭabarānī, *Awsaṭ*, 5664.

13. Ibn Abī Shayba, *Muṣannaf*, 25415; Ibn Abī al-Dunyā, 150; Abū 'Abdal-Rahmān al-Sulamī, *Ādāb al-Ṣuḥba*, 137.

14. Qur'ān, 4:36.

15. Ibn Khuzayma, *Ṣaḥīḥ*, 2067; Ibn Māja, *Sunan*, 1844.

16. Bukhārī, *Ṣaḥīḥ*, 6138.

17. Bukhārī, *Ṣaḥīḥ*, 6019; Muslim, *Ṣaḥīḥ*, 47.

would allow him to inherit.[18]

Preserving ties of kinship and kind behavior towards neighbors will not be complete unless one refrains from harming them, endures their harm, and does good to them according to the means at one's disposal. He has said, may blessings and peace be upon him and his family, *He who is preserving* [*his kinship ties*] *is not he who rewards* [*acts of goodness*]*; rather, it is he who, when his kinship ties are severed, rejoins them.*[19] And, *Habituate yourselves to kindness when people behave kindly, but do not wrong them when they behave badly.*[20]

And success is by God.

---

18. Bukhārī, *Ṣaḥīḥ*, 6015; Muslim, *Ṣaḥīḥ*, 2624. Allowing the neighbor a share in inheriting would imply an extremely close relationship, equal to that between blood kin.

19. Bukhārī, *Ṣaḥīḥ*, 5991; Abū Dāwūd, *Sunan*, 1697.

20. Tirmidhī, *Sunan*, 2007; Bazzār, *Musnad,* 2802.

Chapter 24

On Kindness and Charity

You must love and hate only for the sake of God, for this is one of the firmest handholds of faith. The Messenger of God—may God's blessings and peace be upon him—has said, *The best of deeds are love and hate for the sake of God the Exalted.*[1] When you love the servant who is obedient to God because of his obedience, and hate the one who is disobedient to God because of his disobedience, and not for any other reason, then you are one who truly loves and hates for God. If you find in yourself no love for the people of goodness because of their goodness, and no loathing for the people of evil because of their evil, then know that your faith is weak.

You must keep the company of the best of people and avoid that of the worst; sit with the virtuous and avoid the unjust. The Prophet has said, may God's blessings and peace be upon him and his family, *A man's religion is that of his intimates, so let each of you consider who to be intimate with.*[2] And he has said, may blessings and peace be upon him and his family, *A good companion is better than solitude, and solitude is better than an evil companion.*[3] Know that associating with people of goodness and keeping their company implants the love of goodness in the heart and helps to practice it, while associating with the people of evil and keeping their company implants the love of evil and the love of practicing it in the heart. He who associates closely with a particular group of people inevitably ends up loving them, whether they are good or evil, and a man is with those he loves[4] both in this world and the next.

1. Abū Dāwūd, *Sunan*, 4599.
2. Aḥmad, *Musnad,* 8417; Abū Dāwūd, *Sunan*, 4833; Tirmidhī, *Sunan*, 2379.
3. Al-Ḥākim, *Mustadrak*, 5466; Bayhaqī, *Shu'ab al-Īmān,* 4639; Al-Shihāb, *Musnad*. 1266.
4. Bukhārī, *Ṣaḥīḥ*, 6168; Muslim, *Ṣaḥīḥ*, 2640.

You must be merciful to the servants of God and compassionate to His creatures, and be gentle and kind, of engaging manners and easy to approach. Beware of being callous, coarse, obscene, or difficult to approach. The Prophet has said, may God's blessings and peace be upon him and his family, *God is Merciful to those of His servants who are merciful;*[5] *those who show no mercy are shown no mercy.*[6] And, *A believer is affable and easy to approach; there is no good in he who is neither affable nor easy to approach.*[7]

You must teach the ignorant, guide those who stray, remind the distracted, and beware of neglecting any of these, saying, "Only those who possess knowledge and practice it can teach and remind; I am not one of them." "I am not worthy to guide others, for such is the attribute of the great." This is nothing but satanic deceit, for teaching and reminding are part of practicing what one knows, and great men only become great by the grace of God and their guiding God's servants to His path. If you are unworthy now, then the only way to become worthy is to do good and invite others to it. Evil lies only in making claims and leading others to other than the truth.

You must comfort the broken-hearted, be gentle to the weak and the needy, console the poor, be lenient to the insolvent, and lend to those who ask you. *The reward for a loan exceeds that for charity eighteen times. This is because the loan is taken only by one in need.*[8] Console those who are stricken by adversity, for the Prophet has said, may God's blessings and peace be upon him and his family, *He who consoles a man stricken by adversity,* [thus helping him to endure patiently], *receives a similar reward.*[9]

Beware of gloating, which is to rejoice at another Muslim's misfortune, for he has said, may blessings and peace be upon him and his family, *Never gloat openly at your brother, lest God relieve him and afflict you.*[10]

---

5. Bukhārī, *Ṣaḥīḥ*, 7448; Ibn Ḥibbān, *Ṣaḥīḥ*, 461.
6. Bukhārī, *Ṣaḥīḥ*, 5997; Muslim, *Ṣaḥīḥ*, 2318.
7. Bayhaqī, *Shu'ab al-Īmān,* 7252, 7766; Aḥmad, *Musnad,* 9198, 22840.
8. Ibn Māja, *Sunan*, 2431; Bayhaqī, *Shu'ab al-Īmān,* 3286, 3288.
9. Tirmidhī, *Sunan*, 1073; Ibn Māja, *Sunan*, 1602.
10. Bayhaqī, *Shu'ab al-Īmān,* 6355.

Beware of reviling a Muslim for a sin he has fallen into, for he who does so will not die before being likewise afflicted.

You must relieve those in hardship, fulfil the needs of those in need, and keep the sinner's disgrace concealed. For he has said, may blessings and peace be upon him and his family, *God shall grant ease to him who eases the hardship of another, and shall conceal, in this world and the hereafter,* [*the sins*] *of him who conceals* [*the disgrace of*] *a believer; and He shall relieve from one of the hardships of Resurrection Day he who relieves a Muslim from one of the hardships of this world; and He shall fulfill the need of he who fulfills his brother's need. God assists His servant so long as he is assisting his brother.*[11]

You must remove all causes of harm from the Muslim's road, for this is one of the branches of faith. A *ḥadīth* says, *I saw a man walking freely in the Garden because of a tree that used to harm people on the road, and he had cut it down.*[12]

You must show compassion to the orphan and stroke his head, for he has said, may peace be upon him, *He who strokes an orphan's head, God records a good deed for each hair that his hand has touched.*[13]

Try to gladden the hearts of believers in every possible way, provided these ways are not sinful. You must intercede for anyone who requests it of you with those with whom you have influence, for God will ask His servant to account for his influence just as He will ask him to account for his money. But if a servant falls liable to a statutory punishment [*ḥadd*] such as that pertaining to illegal intercourse or theft, then beware of interceding on his behalf, for intercession in respect of statutory punishments is not permissible. If, following your intercession, you should receive a gift for it, then refuse it, for it is a form of bribery.

You must always smile at believers, show them an engaging friendly face, speak well to them, be gentle and 'lower your wing' [14]

11. Muslim, *Ṣaḥīḥ*, 2580, 2699; Tirmidhī, *Sunan*, 1930; Abū Dāwūd, *Sunan*, 4946.

12. Muslim, *Ṣaḥīḥ*, 1914.

13. Bayhaqī, *Shu'ab al-Īmān,* 10525; Abū Nu'aym, *Ḥilyat al-Awliyā'*, 8:179.

14. To lower one's wing is to be humble, gentle, compassionate, and responsive.

to them. God the Exalted has said to His Prophet, ***And lower your wing to the believers.***[15] And he has said, may blessings and peace be upon him and his family, *Disdain no act of goodness, even if only to meet your brother with a friendly face.*[16] And he has said, may blessings and peace be upon him and his family, *A kind word is a charity.*[17] It has been handed down that when two Muslims meet and shake hands a hundred mercies are divided between them, ninety-nine of which go to the friendlier of the two.

Beware of breaking off relations with a Muslim for personal reasons. If you need to break off with him for a religious reason then for no more than three days, for he has said, may blessings and peace be upon him and his family, *He who deserts his brother for more than three days will be cast by God into the Fire, unless God succors him with His generosity.*[18] This concerns breaking off for the purpose of discipline; but if it is because a wrong is being committed or a right neglected, then there can be no restoration until he reverts to right conduct.

You must show delight and pleasure when something good befalls the Muslims, such as the arrival of rains, lowering of prices, or victory over aggressors or disbelievers. You must be sad and aggrieved when hardship befalls them such as epidemics, rising prices, and seditions. Entreat God to relieve them of such trials, even while accepting His decree and ordinance. The Messenger of God—may God's blessings and peace be upon him—has said, *He who takes no interest in the affairs of the Muslims is not one of them.*[19] And he has said, may blessings and peace be upon him and his family, *The believers are, in their mutual affection and sympathy, like a body; when one of its organs falls ill, the rest of the body responds with sleeplessness and fever.*[20]

When a Muslim does you a favor, you must accept, thank, and reward him for it. If you cannot reward him, or you fear to

15. Qur'ān, 15:88.
16. Muslim, *Ṣaḥīḥ*, 2626; Tirmidhī, *Sunan*, 1833.
17. Bukhārī, *Ṣaḥīḥ*, 6023; Ibn Khuzayma, *Ṣaḥīḥ*, 1494.
18. Ṭabarānī, *Kabīr*, 815; Ibn Abī Shayba, *Muṣannaf*, 25371.
19. Bayhaqī, *Shu'ab al-Īmān,* 10102; Ṭabarānī, *Ṣaghīr*, 9075; Al-Ḥākim, *Mustadrak,* 7889, 7902.
20. Bukhārī, *Ṣaḥīḥ*, 6011; Muslim, *Ṣaḥīḥ*, 2586.

offend him, then pray for him, for he has said, may blessings and peace be upon him and his family, *Were I to be invited to a foreleg or a trotter I would accept; and were I to be given a foreleg or a trotter as a gift I would accept.*[21] And he has said, may blessings and peace be upon him and his family, *When someone does you a favor reward him; if you are unable to, then pray for him until you feel you have rewarded him sufficiently.*[22] And, *He who says to someone who has done him a favor, "May God reward you with goodness!" has prayed for him exceedingly well.*[23]

Never break a Muslim's heart by refusing what he offers you, for you know that anything that comes to you through him is in reality from God and he is only His powerless and impelled means. A *ḥadīth* says, *He who is given something he has neither asked nor longed for should accept and not refuse it, for it is provision that God has sent him.*[24] A great disadvantage attaches to refusal, namely that the common folk are accustomed to respecting those who refuse their gifts, and it may be that some devout people are motivated in their refusal by the wish to display asceticism so that they be thought highly of, which is why a certain authority used ostensibly to accept, and then secretly dispose charitably of such gifts. However, refusal may become obligatory or recommended in some situations, such as the following:

Something may be given you which you either know or have seen evidence that it is unlawful, or *Zakāt* may be given you on the assumption that you deserve it when you do not.

The giver may be unjust, and persistently so, and you fear that if you accept his favor your heart will lean toward him and away from what is right.

You may understand from the person's behavior that he means by his favors to lead you away from the way of God by means of causing you to assist him in committing an injustice or neglecting a right. Of this nature is anything taken by a judge, a governor, or any other man in authority, from either one or both litigants in a case lodged before them. This is prohibited bribery.

---

21. Bukhārī, *Ṣaḥīḥ*, 2568; Nasā'ī, al-*Sunan al-Kubrā*, 6574.
22. Abū Dāwūd, *Sunan*, 1672; Nasā'ī, *Sunan*, 2567.
23. Tirmidhī, *Sunan*, 2035.
24. Ibn Ḥibbān, *Ṣaḥīḥ*, 3404; Aḥmad, *Musnad*, 17936.

You must therefore refuse [any gifts given] under any of the above-mentioned circumstances. There are other forms which are mentioned elsewhere in the relevant chapters.

Beware of making *du'ā'* against yourself, your children, or any other Muslim, even if they have wronged you. He who prays against those who have wronged him shall have his prayer answered. *Never pray against yourselves, your children, or your wealth, for your prayer may coincide with a time when prayers are answered.*[25]

Beware of unjustly harming a Muslim or insulting him, for he has said, may God's blessings and peace be upon him and his family, *He who hurts a Muslim hurts me, and he who hurts me hurts God.*[26] And, *To insult a Muslim is corruption and to fight him is disbelief.*[27]

Beware of cursing a Muslim, an animal, a servant, or a specific person, even if a disbeliever, unless you know for certain that he has died a disbeliever, as in the cases of Pharaoh and Abū Jahl, or that God's mercy will under no circumstance ever reach him, as in the case of Satan. Know that the curse uttered by a person ascends toward heaven, but finding the gates locked before it, it descends back to earth, the gates of which are also locked before it, so it goes to the one who was cursed, and either finds him vulnerable to it, or else recoils against he who has uttered it.

You must effect reconciliation between the hearts of the believers and cause them to love each other by bringing to light their virtues and concealing their vices. You must restore good relations between them, for such a thing is more meritorious than supererogatory prayers and fasts, especially when effected between a father and his son, or a man and his relatives. God the Exalted says, ***The believers are but brothers; therefore, make peace between your two brothers*.**[28]

Beware of sowing discord through talebearing, backbiting or anything else such as will result in antagonism and aversion; for

25. Muslim, *Ṣaḥīḥ*, 3009; Abū Dāwūd, *Sunan*, 1532.

26. Ṭabarānī, *Ṣaghīr*, 468; *Awsaṭ*, 3607.

27. This version is in Aḥmad, *Musnad,* 4176; Tirmidhī, *Sunan*, 2634. A slightly different version is to be found in Bukhārī and Muslim.

28. Qur'ān, 49:9.

this is considered a formidable sin by God.

Talebearing is to report the words of one person to another with the intention of sowing discord between them. He has said, may God's blessings and peace be upon him and his family, *A talebearer never enters the Garden.*[29] And he has said, may peace be upon him, *The most abhorrent amongst you to God are those who damage* [*relationships*] *by talebearing and create rifts between brethren.*[30]

As for backbiting, it is to say things about a person, in his absence, which he would have resented had he been present, with defamatory intent, whether this defamation is verbal, written, or hinted at. The Messenger of God—may God's blessings and peace be upon him—has said, *Everything about a Muslim is sacrosanct to other Muslims: his blood, his wealth, and his honor.*[31] And he has said, may peace be upon him, *Backbiting is worse than adultery.*[32]

God revealed to Moses, may peace be upon him, "He who dies having repented of backbiting will be the last to enter the Garden, and he who dies persisting in it will be the first to enter the Fire."

Beware of injustice, for it will be darkness on Resurrection Day, especially injustice to others, which is never disregarded by God. The Messenger of God—may God's blessings and peace be upon him—has said, *The bankrupt in my community is he who comes on Resurrection Day with prayers, fasts, and* Zakāt, *but had struck someone, insulted someone, taken someone's money, spilled someone's blood, and beaten someone. This one will take from his good deeds and that one will take from his good deeds. When his good deeds are exhausted before he has settled their due some of their evil deeds will be taken and added to his, after which he will be cast into the Fire.*[33] Therefore, if ever you wrong anyone, hasten to escape from the situation by submitting to punish-

29. Muslim, *Ṣaḥīḥ*, 105; Aḥmad, *Musnad,* 23325.

30. Ṭabarānī, *Ṣaghīr*, 835; *Awsaṭ*, 7697.

31. Muslim, *Ṣaḥīḥ*, 2564; Abū Dāwūd, *Sunan*, 4882.

32. Bayhaqī, *Shu'ab al-Īmān,* 6315; Ṭabarānī, *Awsaṭ*, 6590.

33. Muslim, *Ṣaḥīḥ*, 2581; Bayhaqī, *Shu'ab al-Īmān,* 338; Aḥmad, *Musnad*, 8842.

ment if it is an offence involving his person, asking to be absolved if it is a matter of honor, and returning what you have taken if it is a financial injustice. A *ḥadīth* says, *He who commits an injustice against his brother should ask him to absolve him before the day when there shall be neither Dīnār nor Dirham; before his brother is given of his good deeds, and if he has none, his brother's evil deeds will be cast upon him.*[34] If you find yourself altogether unable to make reparations for some of your injustices, then seek refuge in God with sincerity and urgency, and acknowledge your powerlessness, that He may get your adversary to accept you; also make *du'ā'* in abundance and ask forgiveness for those whom you have wronged.

You must defend the lives, honor, and wealth of all Muslims as you defend your own, whether in their presence or absence; for he who supports a Muslim will be supported by God, and he who deserts a Muslim will be deserted by Him.

---

34. Bukhārī, *Ṣaḥīḥ*, 6534.

Chapter 25

On Counsel

You must be of good counsel to all Muslims. The summit of this is that you conceal nothing from them which if known would either bring about something good or preserve from something evil. The Messenger of God has said, may God's blessings and peace be upon him and his family, *Religion is good counsel.*[1] Part of this is to be for a Muslim in his absence just as you are in his presence, and not to give him more verbal signs of affection than you have for him in your heart. It is also part of this that when a Muslim seeks your advice, and you know that the correct course does not lie in that which he is inclined to do, you should tell him so.

The absence of good counsel is indicated by the presence of jealousy for the favors God has given others. The origin of such jealousy is that you find it intolerable that God has granted one of His servants a good thing, whether religious or worldly. Its maximum is to wish that he be deprived of it. It has been handed down that, *Jealousy consumes good deeds just as fire consumes dry wood.*[2] The jealous person is in fact objecting to God's management of His Dominion, as if he were saying, "O Lord, you have placed your favors where they do not belong."

It is permitted, however, to be envious without resentment, whereby when you see a favor of God bestowed on one of His servants, you ask Him—Transcendent is He—to grant you the same.

Whenever someone praises you, you must dislike his praises in your heart. If he has praised you for something that is really yours, say, "Praise is God's alone, for He reveals the good things and conceals the ugly ones." But if he has praised you for something which is not yours, say as one of our predecessors has said, "O God, do not call me to account for what they say, forgive me what they do not know, and make me better than they think!"

---

1. Muslim, *Ṣaḥīḥ*, 55; Abū Dāwūd, *Sunan*, 4944.
2. Abū Dāwūd, *Sunan*, 4944; Ibn Māja, *Sunan*, 4210.

As for you, never praise anyone unless you know that your praises will incite him to more good works or that he is a superior man whose superiority is not well known and you wish to make it so, on condition that you keep yourself safe from lying and he from conceit.

When you wish to give advice to someone regarding a particular behavior of his that you have come to know about, you must talk to him privately and tactfully, and never state explicitly what can be alluded to discreetly. Should he ask you, "Who reported this to you?" then do not tell him lest you stir up enmity. If he accepts [your advice], praise and thank God; if he does not, then blame yourself and say, "O evil soul, it is because of you that I was defeated! Think! For you may not have fulfilled the conditions and proprieties necessary for giving advice."

If you are given something as a trust, guard it better than if it were your own. You must return whatever is entrusted to you and beware of betraying that trust. The Messenger of God—may God's blessings and peace be upon him—has said, *He has no faith who is untrustworthy.*[3] And, *Three* [*things*] *are clinging to the Throne: Benefaction, which says, 'O God, I exist only by you, let me not be denied!' Kinship ties, which say, 'O God, I exist only by you, let me not be severed!' and Trust, which says, 'O God, I exist only by you, let me not be betrayed*!"[4]

You must speak truthfully and honor your commitments and your promises, for breaching commitments and breaking promises are signs of hypocrisy. *The signs of a hypocrite are three: when he speaks, he lies; when he promises, he breaks his promise; and when he is trusted, he betrays that trust.*[5] And in another version, *and when he makes a pledge, he breaks it; and when he quarrels, he acts outrageously.*[6]

You must be wary of argumentation and wrangling, for they arouse rancor in the breasts of men, alienate hearts, and lead to

3. Aḥmad, *Musnad*, 12383; Ibn Ḥibbān, *Ṣaḥīḥ*, 194.

4. Bazzār, Musnad, 4181; Bayhaqī, Shu'ab al-Īmān, 7564. "I am by you!" means: You gave me such an honorable position in the proximity of Your Throne, therefore let me not be misused, for, close to you as I am, the consequences will be terrible.

5. Bukhārī, *Ṣaḥīḥ*, 33, 2682; Muslim, *Ṣaḥīḥ*, 59.

6. Bukhārī, *Ṣaḥīḥ*, 2459; Muslim, *Ṣaḥīḥ*, 58.

enmity and hatred. If anyone argues against you and has right on his side, you must accept what he says, for the truth must always be submitted to. If, on the other hand, he is wrong, then leave him, for he is ignorant, and God the Exalted has said, ***And turn away from the ignorant.***[7]

You must abandon all joking; if very occasionally you do joke to assuage a Muslim's heart, then speak only the truth. The Messenger of God, may God's blessings and peace be upon him, has said, *Neither quarrel with your brother nor jest, and never make him a promise, then break it.*[8]

You must respect all Muslims, especially people of merit among them such as scholars, the virtuous, the noble, and those whose hair has greyed in Islam.

Never frighten or alarm a Muslim; never mock, ridicule, or despise him, for these are ominous and blameworthy behaviors. The Messenger of God—may God's blessings and peace be upon him—has said, *It is sufficient evil for a man that he should despise his brother Muslim.*[9]

You must be humble, for humility is the attribute of believers. Beware of pride, for God does not like the proud. Those who humble themselves are elevated by God, while those who are proud are abased by Him. The Messenger of God—may God's blessings and peace be upon him—has said, *He will not enter the Garden in whose heart is an atom's weight of pride.*[10] And, *Pride is to deny the truth and despise other people.*[11] He is proud who looks at himself with admiration and at others with disdain.

There are signs which distinguish the humble from the proud, ***that God may separate the vile from the good.***[12] Signs of humility include a liking for obscurity, a dislike of fame, an acceptance of truth whether it be from a man of high or low birth, loving the poor, associating with them and keep their company, fulfilling the rights of your brothers upon you as completely as you can, thank-

7. Qur'ān, 7:199.
8. Bukhārī, *al-Adab al-Mufrad*, 394; Tirmidhī, *Sunan*, 1995.
9. Muslim, *Ṣaḥīḥ*, 2564; Abū Dāwūd, *Sunan*, 4882.
10. Muslim, *Ṣaḥīḥ*, 91; Tirmidhī, *Sunan*, 1999.
11. Bukhārī, *al-Adab al-Mufrad*, 556; Muslim, *Ṣaḥīḥ*, 91; Tirmidhī, *Sunan*, 1995.
12. Qur'ān, 8:37.

ing those of them who fulfill their duties to you, and excusing those who are remiss. Signs of pride include desiring to be seated in the most eminent place when in company or in a public gathering, praising and vaunting oneself, speaking pompously, flaunting the merits of one's forefathers, strutting, and neglecting the rights of your brothers, while demanding yours.

Chapter 26

On Salutations and a Salutary Opinion

You must greet all Muslims with *salām*, both those you know and those you do not. If you greet someone and he does not return your greeting, do not think ill of him, but rather say to yourself, "He may not have heard, or perhaps he did answer and it is I who did not hear."

When you enter your house greet your family with *salām*, and when you enter an empty mosque or house say, "*As-salāmu 'alaynā wa-'alā 'ibādi'llāhi' ṣ-ṣāliḥīn.*" [May peace be upon us and upon the virtuous servants of God.]

When you meet a Muslim always try to greet him first. The Messenger of God—may blessings and peace be upon him—was once asked, "When two men meet, which of them should greet the other first?" He replied, *The one most devoted to God.*[1] And in another *ḥadīth* he said that it was the rider who should greet the pedestrian, the man standing should greet the man seated, the younger man the older one, and the smaller group the larger.[2]

When someone sneezes and then praises God, you must say to him, "*Yarḥamuka'llāh.*" [May God have mercy on you.] If he fails to praise God, then remind him by saying, "*Al-ḥamdu li-llāh.*" [God be praised.]

You must not enter a house other than yours without asking permission; if you ask thrice and receive no answer, then ask no more [and depart].

When a Muslim calls you, answer with: "*Labbayk!*" [At your service!] If he invites you to his table, accept, unless you have a legitimate excuse. If he adjures you, allow him to fulfill his oath so long as it does not involve anything sinful. Never beseech any-

1. Tirmidhī, *Sunan*, 2694.
2. Abū Dāwūd, *Sunan*, 5199; Tirmidhī, *Sunan*, 2703.

one by God, but if you are beseeched, comply. The Messenger of God—may blessings and peace be upon him—said, *Accursed is he who is beseeched by God and refuses.*[3]

You must visit the sick, escort funerals, and visit your brothers in God whenever you feel you miss them. Shake their hands when you meet, inquire about how they and those who are not there at the time are, so that if any of them is sick you may visit him, or if any of them is working on something you may help if you can or else pray for him.

You must think well of all Muslims, and beware of thinking ill of any of them. He has said, may God's blessings and peace be upon him and his family, *Two traits are unsurpassed by any other good: thinking well of God, and thinking well of His servants. And two traits are unsurpassed by any other evil: thinking ill of God, and thinking ill of His servants.*[4] To think well of Muslims is to regard nothing they do or say as evil if it can be interpreted otherwise. If you cannot find a good interpretation, as in the case of sins for example, then to think well of them is to reproach them for committing them, but believe that their faith will eventually drive them to give over and repent. To think ill of Muslims is to regard as evil those acts and words of theirs which are in appearance good. For example, you may see a Muslim who frequently prays, gives charity, and recites [the Qur'ān], but think that he is only doing so that people may see him, and that his aim is wealth and social eminence. This corrupt form of thinking occurs to those only who are inwardly vile and is an attribute of hypocrites. As God the Exalted says in describing them, ***Those who point disparagingly at such of the believers who willingly give charity,***[5] that is, who accuse them of ostentation. And He also says, ***The hypocrites try to deceive God, but it is He who will deceive them. When they rise to the Prayer, they rise lazily, making a show for the people.***[6]And he has said, may peace be upon him, *Invoke*

3. Ṭabarānī, *Kabīr*, 943.

4. This saying, here presumed to be a *ḥadīth*, is sometimes quoted by scholars, Qur'ān exegetes, and Sufis, such as Shaykh Ibn 'Ajība in *al-Baḥr al-Madīd*, 1: 154; and Shaykh Zarrūq in *al-Naṣīḥa al-Kāfiya*, p. 15, but is nowhere to be found in currently available compilations of *ḥadīth*.

5. Qur'ān, 9:79.

6. Qur'ān, 4: 142

God in such abundance that the hypocrites will say that you are ostentatious![7]

You must make frequent supplications, and ask forgiveness for yourself, your parents, relatives, and friends in particular, and all other Muslims in general, for the prayer of a Muslim for his brother in his absence is answered. He has said, may blessings and peace be upon him and his family, *Some prayers have no veils between them and God: the prayers of the wronged and of the Muslim for his brother in his absence.*[8] And he has said, may peace be upon him, *When a Muslim prays for his brother in his absence, the angel says, "Amīn, and the same for you!"*[9] Maymūn ibn Mihrān—may God have mercy on him—said, "He who asks forgiveness for his parents after each obligatory prayer has thanked them as he was ordered to do in His saying, Exalted is He, ***Thank Me and your two parents***."[10] It has been related that the one who asks forgiveness twenty-seven times a day for "all believing men and women" will be among those whose prayers are answered and through whom people are given provision and rain, and these are the attributes of the saints.[11]

Know that there are for Muslims many mutual obligations. If you want to fulfill these properly then behave towards Muslims, whether they are present or absent, as you would like them to behave towards you. Oppose your own soul: accustom your heart to wish for them every good that you wish for yourself and detest for them every evil that you detest for yourself. The Messenger of God—may God's blessings and peace be upon him—has said, *None of you believes until he loves for his brother that which he loves for himself.*[12] And he has said, may blessings and peace be upon him and his family, *Muslims are to one another as a single building, each part of which supports the others,*[13] *and as one*

7. Bayhaqī, *Shu'ab al-Īmān*, 524; Aḥmad ibn Ḥanbal, *Kitāb al-Zuhd,* 557; Ibn al-Mubārak, *Kitāb al-Zuhd wa'l-Raqā'iq*, 1022.

8. Ṭabarānī, *Du'ā'*, 1319, 1330; *Kabīr*, 11232.

9. Muslim, *Ṣaḥīḥ*, 2732; Abū Dāwūd, *Sunan*, 1534.

10. Qur'ān, 31:14.

11. Suyūṭī, *al-Jāmi' al-Ṣaghīr*, 12182; Haythamī, *Majma' al-Zawā'id,* 17600; Ibn Kathīr, *Jāmi' al-Masānīd wa'l-Sunan*, 12126.

12. Bukhārī, *Ṣaḥīḥ*, 13; Muslim, *Ṣaḥīḥ*, 71.

13. Bukhārī, *Ṣaḥīḥ*, 481; Muslim, *Ṣaḥīḥ*, 2585.

body, which when one of its organs suffers the rest of the body suffers with it.[14] And Yaḥyā ibn Mu'ādh—may God have mercy on him—said, "If you cannot be of benefit to the Muslims, then do not harm them; if you cannot please them, then do not abuse them; if cannot make them happy, then do not make them sad; and if you cannot praise them, then do not disparage them." My master Muḥyiddīn 'Abd al-Qādir al-Jīlānī—may God be pleased with him—said, "Be with the Truth as if [there were] no creation, and be with creation as if [you had] no ego." And one of our ancestors said, "People are either afflicted or free [from affliction], so be compassionate to the afflicted and thank God for freedom [from affliction]."

And praise belongs to God, Lord of the Worlds.

14. Muslim, *Ṣaḥīḥ*, 2586; Aḥmad, *Musnad*, 18380.

Chapter 27

On Repentance, Hope, and Fear

You must repent of every single sin, small or great, outward or inward, for repentance is the first step that a servant takes on the Path, and is the foundation of all other stations; and God loves the penitent. He says, Exalted is He, ***God loves those who are ever repentant and He loves those who purify themselves.***[1] And He says, Transcendent and Exalted is He, ***Repent to God entirely, O believers, that you may succeed.***[2] And the Messenger of God—may God's blessings and peace be upon him—has said, *He who repents from a sin is as if he has not sinned.*[3]

Know that repentance cannot be sound until the sin itself is abandoned, remorse is felt, and one is determined never to repeat it for the rest of one's life. The true penitent is characterized by certain signs, among which are softness of the heart, frequent weeping, adhering to obedience, and forsaking evil companions and places.

Beware of willful persistence, which is to sin and not repent immediately. It is a believer's duty to guard himself against sins, both minor and major, in the way he would against burning fires, engulfing water, or lethal poisons. He should neither commit nor intend a sin, neither talk about it beforehand nor delight in it afterward. If he does fall into one, he should conceal and hate it, and hasten to repent immediately.

You must renew your repentance frequently, for sins are numerous and a servant is never free, outwardly or inwardly, from a great number of rebellious acts, even if his state is good, behavior upright, and obedience continual. It should suffice you [to know] that the Messenger of God—may God's blessings and peace be upon him—infallible and utterly perfect as he was, repented to

1. Qur'ān, 2:222.
2. Qur'ān, 24:31.
3. Ibn Māja, *Sunan*, 4250; Bayhaqī, *Shu'ab al-Īmān*, 6780.

God and asked His forgiveness more than seventy times each day.[4]

You must ask for forgiveness repeatedly, night and day, especially in the last hours of the night. The Messenger of God has said, may God's blessings and peace be upon him and his family, *God will grant the one who perseveres in asking forgiveness relief from every worry, a way out of every difficulty, and provision from whence he does not expect.*[5]

You must say abundantly, "*Rabbi'ghfir lī wa-tub'alayya innaka anta't-tawwābu'r-raḥīm!*" [Lord, forgive me and relent toward me; truly, you are the Ever-Relenting, the Compassionate!] for the Companions used to hear the Messenger of God—may blessings and peace be upon him—utter almost a hundred times this blessed invocation in a single sitting.[6]

Do use the prayer of Dhū al-Nūn,[7] may peace be upon him, ***Lā ilāha illā anta subḥānaka innī kuntu min aẓ-ẓalimīn.***[8] [***There is no god but You, Transcendent are You! I have been one of the unjust.***] For it has been related that it contains God's Supreme Name and that no-one who is worried or aggrieved repeats it but that God grants him relief. God the Exalted says, ***We answered him and rescued him from grief, and in such wise do We rescue the believers.***[9]

You must have hope and fear, for these are the two noblest fruits of certainty, and God has attributed them to the Foremost among His servants. He says, and He is the Most Truthful Speaker, ***Those whom they call seek the way to approach their Lord, which of them shall be the nearest; they hope for His mercy and fear His torment; indeed, the torment of your Lord should be feared.***[10] And the Messenger of God—may God's blessings and peace be upon him—has said, *God the Exalted says, "I am as my servant thinks of Me, so let him think of Me what he will."*[11] And

4. Bukhārī, *Ṣaḥīḥ*, 6307.
5. Abū Dāwūd, *Sunan*, 1518; Ibn Māja, *Sunan*, 3819.
6. Bukhārī, *Al-Adab al-Mufrad*, 618; Abū Dāwūd, *Sunan*, 1516.
7. Dhu'l-Nūn is a name of the Prophet Jonah (Yūnus), may peace be upon him.
8. Qur'ān, 21:87.
9. Qur'ān, 21:88.
10. Qur'ān, 17:57.
11. Ibn Ḥibbān, *Ṣaḥīḥ*, 633; Aḥmad, *Musnad*, 16016.

he has said, may blessings and peace be upon him, *God the Exalted says, "By My might and majesty, I shall not unite two safeties, nor two fears, in My servant. If he feels secure from Me in this world, I shall make him fear on the day I resurrect My servants; but if he fears Me in this world, I shall make him secure on the day I gather them together."* [12]

The basis of hope is the heart's knowledge of the immensity of God's mercy and generosity, the magnitude of His favors and kindness, and His gracious promise to those who obey Him. This knowledge generates a state of joy which is termed "hope," the intended result of which is that one hastens to acts of goodness and is keen to perform all acts of obedience, for obedience is the road to God's Good Pleasure [*Riḍwān*], and His Garden.

As for the basis of fear, it is the heart's knowledge of the majesty of God the Exalted, His invincible might, His independence of any of His creatures, and the severe punishments and painful torments with which He threatens those who disobey Him and contravene His commands. This knowledge generates a state of apprehension which is termed "fear," the intended result of which is that one abandons sins and thoroughly guards oneself against them, for sin is the road leading to God's wrath and His place of punishment.

Any hope or fear that does not lead to adherence to obedience and the renunciation of transgression is considered by the people of inward vision to be nothing but useless and futile illusion, and folly, for he who really hopes for something seeks it and he who really fears something invariably flees from it.

Know that people are [in this respect] of three kinds:

Firstly, a servant who has committed himself to God, feels secure with Him, and the shadows of whose passions have been dispelled by the dawning of the lights of His nearness, so that his only remaining pleasure is to commune with Him, and his only remaining repose to deal with Him. His hope will thus have turned into yearning and love, and his fear into reverence and awe.

Secondly, a servant who feels he is in danger of neglecting his obligations or inclining towards forbidden things; for him,

---

12. Ṭabarānī, *Musnad al-Shāmiyyīn*, 462; Ibn Ḥibbān, *Ṣaḥīḥ*, 640; Bayhaqī, *Shu'ab al-Īmān*, 759.

fear and hope should be in equilibrium, just like the wings of a bird. "Should the fear of a believer and his hope be weighed, they should be equal." This is the state of most believers.

And finally, a servant who is overcome by confusion and heedlessness. What is appropriate for him is constant fear, so that he may be deterred from committing sins. This applies at all times saving that of his death, when hope should predominate, for he has said, may blessings and peace be upon him and his family, *Let none of you die not thinking well of God.*[13]

When you speak of hope with the common people, you must confine yourself to conditional hope; that is, you must mention the gracious promises and abundant rewards dependent on doing good and avoiding sins. Beware of speaking to them of unconditional hope by saying, for example, "The servant sins and the Lord forgives," or, "Were it not for sins, the clemency and forbearance of God would not manifest," or, "Compared with the immensity of God's mercy, all the sins of the ancients and the latecomers are but a drop in a fathomless sea," and other similar things. Such words are true but harmful to the common people, who may be induced to transgress, and you would have been the cause. Not every truth is to be voiced, for there are men appropriate to each degree.

Beware of either despairing of God's mercy or feeling secure from His deception, for both are major sins. He says, Exalted is He, ***Only those despair of the mercy of their Lord who are astray,***[14] ***and none feels secure from God's deception save the losers***.[15]

"Despair" is to be so overwhelmed by fear as to leave absolutely no room for hope, while "security" is to have so much hope as to leave absolutely no room for fear. Both are ignorant of God and will inevitably neglect His obedience and transgress. For he who despairs forsakes obedience because he feels it will avail him nothing, while he who is secure commits sins thinking they will do him no harm. We seek God's protection against damnation and evil destiny.

---

13. Muslim, *Ṣaḥīḥ*, 2877; Abū Dāwūd, *Sunan*, 3113.
14. Qur'ān, 15:56.
15. Qur'ān, 7:99.

Beware of those hopes for forgiveness which sever you from forgiveness. These you hear from deluded people who say that ***God forgives all sins,***[16] that He stands in no need of us and our works, that His treasures are full of bounty and His mercy envelops everything, but who then persist in committing sins and neglecting good works, as though they were in effect saying that acts of obedience are of no benefit and sins bring no harm. This is a formidable falsehood! God the Exalted says, ***He who does an atom's weight of good shall see it, and he who does an atom's weight of evil shall see it.***[17] And He says, Exalted is He, ***To God belongs all that is the heavens and the earth; that He may reward those who did wrong with what they did and reward those who did well with goodness.***[18] And the Messenger of God—may God's blessings and peace be upon him—has said, *The shrewd person is he who accuses himself and works for that which follows death, while the incompetent is he who follows his soul's passions, yet harbors vain hopes in God.*[19] If you say to one of those deluded people that he should refrain from earning and commerce because God the Exalted will send him his provision, he will ridicule you and reply that he never saw anything come except when sought and pursued, mostly with toil and exertion. Notwithstanding that, God the Exalted has guaranteed his share of this world for him, but not the hereafter. Is this anything but an inversion and standing upside down on one's head?

Al-Ḥasan al-Baṣrī—may God have mercy on him—has said, "Hopes for forgiveness have deceived some people until they left this world bankrupt," that is, devoid of good works. And he has said, may God have mercy on him, "The believer conjoins excellent behavior with fear, while the hypocrite conjoins vile behavior with security; for the believer starts his in apprehension and ends it in apprehension. He works and says, 'I shall not be saved, I shall not be saved,' while the hypocrite abandons works and says, 'Most people are like this, I will be forgiven.'" The Prophets and the saints, perfect as they were in their knowledge of God, their good

16. Qur'ān, 39:53.
17. Qur'ān, 94:7, 8.
18. Qur'ān, 53:31.
19. Tirmidhī, *Sunan*, 2459; Ibn Māja, *Sunan*, 4260.

opinions of Him, good works, and scarcity or total lack of sins, were nonetheless exceedingly fearful and apprehensive. ***They are those whom God has guided, so follow their guidance.***[20]

20. Qur'ān, 6:90.

Chapter 28

On Fortitude

You must show fortitude [*ṣabr*],[1] for it is this matter's foundation and necessary as long as you are in this abode. It is a noble trait and a great virtue. God the Exalted says, ***O believers, seek help in fortitude and prayer; for indeed God is with those who have fortitude.***[2] And He says, Exalted is He, ***And we made them leaders guiding by Our command when they had fortitude.***[3] And He says, Exalted is He, ***Indeed those who have fortitude will be paid their wages without stint.***[4] The Messenger of God—may God's blessings and peace be upon him—said that fortitude is the commander of the believer's troops. And he said in his advice to Ibn 'Abbās, *Know that there is much good in patiently enduring that which you find unpleasant, and that victory comes with fortitude, relief with hardship, and with each difficulty comes ease.*[5]

Know that happiness depends on the occurrence of nearness to God, which in turn depends on always following the truth and avoiding falsehood. The ego is inclined, by its very nature, to detest truth and lean towards falsehood. The determination of the seeker of felicity is thus always in need of fortitude, sometimes to force the soul to follow the truth and sometimes to force it to avoid falsehood.

Fortitude is of four kinds:

• Firstly: Patient endurance of acts of obedience. This is realized inwardly by sincerity and presence of the heart, and outwardly by perseverance, constancy, zeal, and correct performance of these acts. This kind of fortitude is helped by remembering

---

1. Ṣabr may mean fortitude, patience, equanimity, or patient endurance, according to the context.
2. Qur'ān, 2:153.
3. Qur'ān, 32:24.
4. Qur'ān, 39:10.
5. Bayhaqī, *Shu'ab al-Īmān*, 1043, 9528; Aḥmad, *Musnad*, 2803.

God's promised rewards, both immediate and to come, for obedience. He who keeps to this kind of fortitude reaches the station of nearness where he will find indescribable sweetness, pleasure, and intimacy in acts of obedience. He to whom this happens must not rely on it, but rather on God.

• Secondly: Patient endurance in renouncing sins. This is realized outwardly by avoiding them and keeping away from the places where they might be committed, and inwardly by preventing the soul from ruminating upon them and inclining to them, for the very beginning of a sin is a thought. As for remembering previous sins, if this results in fear or remorse, it is good, if not, then refraining is better. This kind of fortitude is helped by remembering God's threats of punishment in this world and the next for disobedience. He who keeps to this kind of fortitude will be honored by God with such distaste to all disobedience that entering the Fire would be easier for him than the committal of the smallest sin.

• Thirdly: Patient endurance of unpleasant things. These are of two kinds: the first comprises those which come from God without an intermediary, as for example illness, infirmity, loss of wealth, or the death of dear relatives or friends. [This kind of fortitude] is realized inwardly by forsaking restlessness, which is to become annoyed and irritated, and outwardly by not complaining to any created being. It is not incompatible with describing an illness to a physician, or by one's eyes overflowing with tears at a time of loss, but it is incompatible with slapping one's cheeks, rending one's clothes, wailing, and the like. This kind of fortitude is helped by the knowledge that impatience is painful in itself, in addition to loss of reward and deserving punishment, and that it is foolish to complain to one who can neither benefit nor protect his own self, and such are all created beings. Furthermore, to complain is evidence of not finding one's sufficiency in God, ***in whose hand is the dominion*** [Malakūt] ***of all things,***[6] and also of neglecting to remember those verses which mention the reward of patient endurance of losses, infirmities, and afflictions, and that God the Exalted knows better than a person that which is of most benefit to him. He says, Exalted is He, ***We shall try you with something of fear, hunger, and diminution of wealth, lives,***

6. Qur'ān, 34:83.

and fruits; and give good tidings to those who have patience, who when stricken by hardship say, "We belong to God, and to Him we shall return!' God will send blessings and mercy on them; those are they who are guided.[7] God will give the one who perseveres in this kind of fortitude to taste the sweetness of surrender and find rest in the serenity of contentment [*riḍā*]. We will mention contentment, God willing, in due course.

The second kind of unpleasant things comprises those which are caused by other human beings, whether by way of offences touching oneself, one's honor, or one's money. Complete fortitude in this regard means to prevent oneself from hating the offender, if he is a Muslim, not to wish him harm, to prevent one's tongue from making *du'ā'* to God against him, and to refrain altogether from reproaching him, either through forbearance and fortitude, or relying on God's assistance, or pardon and forgiveness by desiring His reward. This kind of fortitude is helped by knowledge of that which has been handed down regarding the merits of suppressing anger, enduring injuries, and forgiving others. God the Exalted says, ***The wage of he who is forgiving and reconciling falls on God; He does not love the unjust. And whoso defends himself after he has suffered wrong, there is no blame against them. Blame is only for those who oppress men and transgress in the earth without right; for them is a painful torment. But those that endure patiently and forgive, that is the difficult thing indeed.***[8] He has said, may blessings and peace be upon him and his family, *He who suppresses his anger when able to carry out its dictates, God fills his heart with serenity and faith.*[9] And he has said, may peace be upon him, *A herald will call on Resurrection Day, "Let those whose reward fall upon God arise!" and those shall arise who were forgiving of others.*[10]

The one who perseveres in this kind of fortitude will be honored by God with a good character, which is the source of all virtues and the foundation of all perfections. He has said, may blessings and peace be upon him and his family, *Nothing shall*

7. Qur'ān, 2:155, 156, 157.
8. Qur'ān, 42:40, 41, 42, 43.
9. Al-Shihāb, *Musnad*, 437; Ibn Abī 'Āsim, *Al-Āḥād wa al-Mathānī*, 2649.
10. Ṭabarānī, *Awsaṭ*, 1998; Abū Nu'aym, *Ḥilyat al-Awliyā'*, 6:187.

weigh more heavily in the Balance than a good character; a servant may attain through his good character the rank of the one who is ever praying and fasting.[11] And he has said, may peace be upon him, *Those I love most and who will sit closest to me on Resurrection Day are those among you who are the best in character.*[12] Ibn al-Mubārak—may God the Exalted have mercy on him—said, "Good character is to show an engaging face, be generous with good works, and refrain from doing harm." And Imām al-Ghazālī—may God spread his benefit—said, "Good character is a disposition deeply ingrained in the soul from which beautiful acts spring spontaneously."

• Fourthly: Patient renunciation of appetites, which are all those worldly things to which the soul inclines. Perfect fortitude here is attained by inwardly stopping the soul from thinking and leaning towards them, and outwardly restraining it from seeking or approaching them. This kind of fortitude is helped by knowledge of how the quest for appetites and their actual satisfaction cause distraction from God and His worship, expose one to the risks of falling into suspect and prohibited things, and aid the escalation of greed for this world and the wish to remain therein and enjoy its pleasures. Abū Sulaymān al-Dārānī—may God have mercy on him—has said, "To abandon a single desire is of more benefit to the heart than a year's worship." God will honor he who grows accustomed to denying himself his desires by removing their love from his heart until he attains the state described by a certain Knower, who said, "My desire is that I should desire, so that I may resist my desire, and thus be rid of desire."

And providential success is from God!

---

11. Tirmidhī, *Sunan*, 2003; Bazzār, *Musnad*, 4098.
12. Bukhārī, *al-Adab al-Mufrad*, 272; Aḥmad, *Musnad*, 6735.

Chapter 29

On Gratitude

You must thank God for all that He has favored you with. None of the blessings you possess, whether outward or inward, religious or worldly, comes from other than Him. He says, Exalted is He, ***Whatever good thing you have is from God.***[1] God's favors upon you are far more than you are able to reckon or be aware of, let alone adequately thank Him for. ***If you would count the favors of God, you cannot number them.***[2] Should the poor and the sick among the people of *Tawḥīd* reflect on God's favors upon them, they would become so occupied with giving thanks that they would cease to feel the hardship of patient endurance. Therefore, you should exert yourself to the utmost to thank your Lord, and then confess your incapacity to ever do so adequately.

Know that thankfulness leads to the perpetuation of favors already received and is the means to procure others yet to be obtained. God the Exalted says, ***If you give thanks, I shall surely increase you.***[3] He is too generous to take away a favor from one who is thanking Him. He says, Exalted is He, ***That is because God never changes a blessing He has bestowed on any people until they first change that which is in themselves,***[4] that is by neglecting to give thanks. And God repeatedly exhorts His servants to render thanks to Him in His Book. He says, Exalted is He, ***Eat of the good things with which We have provided you, and give thanks to God if it is truly Him that you worship.***[5] And He says, Exalted is He,

1. Qur'ān, 16:53.
2. Qur'ān, 14:34.
3. Qur'ān, 14:7.
4. Qur'ān, 8:51.
5. Qur'ān, 2:172.

Eat of the provision of your Lord and give thanks to Him.[6] And he has said, may blessings and peace be upon him and his family, *Let each of you have an invoking tongue and a thankful heart.*[7] And, *Faith is of two halves: one is patience and the other thankfulness.*[8]

Know that just as you must thank God for favors which are proper to you, such as knowledge and health, you must also thank Him for favors which are general, such as the sending of Messengers, the revelation of Scriptures, raising up the sky, and stretching out the earth.

And know that if the heart is aware of such favors, that they are from God alone, and that nothing comes to one through one's own ability and power, but only through God's grace and mercy, this is thankfulness. It becomes complete when you use every one of His favors in His obedience, for if you fail to do so you will have neglected to give thanks for them, and if you use them to disobey Him, you will have fallen into ingratitude, at which time favors turn into afflictions. He who still enjoys some favors while using them in disobedience to God is being lured. God the Exalted says, ***We shall lure them from whence they do not know.***[9] And, ***We only give them rein that they may increase in sinfulness.***[10] A *ḥadīth* says, *God gives rein to the wrongdoer until, when He seizes him, He never lets him go.*[11]

It is part of thankfulness to praise God frequently and rejoice for the favors bestowed because they are means of attaining to the nearness of God, as well as evidence of His solicitude for His servant.

It is also part of thankfulness to make much of His favors, even those that are small. It is related that God once said to one of His Prophets, "Whenever I grant you a decaying grain of wheat, know that I have remembered you thereby, and thank Me for it."

---

6. Qur'ān, 34:15.
7. Bayhaqī, *Shu'ab al-Īmān*, 584; Aḥmad, *Musnad*, 23101.
8. Bayhaqī, *Shu'ab al-Īmān*, 9264; Al-Shihāb, *Musnad*, 159.
9. Qur'ān, 7:182.
10. Qur'ān, 3:178.
11. Muslim, *Ṣaḥīḥ*, 2583; Ibn Māja, *Sunan*, 4018.

It is part of thankfulness likewise to speak of God's favors, on condition, however, of never digressing into anything suggesting self-righteousness in religious matters or conceit in worldly matters. Deeds are valued only according to the intentions behind them and all good comes from following our virtuous predecessors in every kind of situation; and God knows best.

Chapter 30

On Detachment

You must detach yourself from this world, for detachment is the forerunner of felicity, the manifestation of solicitude, and the sign of sanctity. Just as loving the world is at the origin of all sins, so also is hating it at the origin of all obedience and excellence. It is sufficient to detach you from the world to know that in numerous passages in His Book, God calls it the ***Comfort of Illusion,***[1] and that al-Ḥasan—may God have mercy on him—said, "The *Comfort of Illusion* is like the green color of vegetation and the toys of girls."[2] And Abū Ṭālib al-Makkī—may God have mercy on him—said, "The *Comfort of Illusion* is a name for rotting carrion." And God the Exalted defines the world as no more than distraction and play to which no intelligent person should pay attention and to which only ignorant fools are attracted. He says, Exalted is He, ***The life of the world is nothing but play and distraction.***[3]

Know that to renounce the world is an immediate felicity and that only those are capable of it whose breasts God has expanded by the dawning of the lights of direct knowledge and certainty. He has said, may blessings and peace be upon him and his family, *When light enters the heart, it expands for it and dilates.* They said, "Is there any sign for that?" He replied, *Yes, to shun the*

---

1. ***The life of this world is but comfort of illusion.*** [Qur'ān, 3:185.] ***Know that the life of this world is only play, distraction, ornaments, boasting among you, and rivalry in wealth and children. It is as a rain whose vegetation pleases the disbelievers, then it withers and you see it turning yellow, then it becomes broken straw; and in the hereafter is a terrible punishment, and forgiveness from God, and His good pleasure. The life of this world is but the comfort of illusion.*** [Qur'ān, 57:20.]

2. Green vegetation looks beautiful but easily turns into dry straw. As for girls' dolls, they are treated as though they are alive when they are really a deceitful appearance of life devoid of any reality, to be toyed with for a while, then discarded.

3. Qur'ān, 6:32.

abode of illusion and attend to the abode of immortality.[4] And he said, peace be upon him, *Detachment from the world relieves the heart and the body, while desire for the world increases worry and sorrow.*[5] And he said, peace be upon him, *Renounce the world, and God will love you.*[6]

The origin of detachment is the heart's knowledge of how vile and insignificant this world really is, that *had it been worth to God so much as a gnat's wing, He would not have given a disbeliever a sip of its water;*[7] that *it is accursed and all that it contains except that which is for the sake of God;*[8] and that *he who takes more than the necessary from it is unwittingly bringing about his own destruction.*[9] The intended result of such knowledge is inwardly to abandon all desire for the world, and outwardly to abandon indulging its pleasures.

The lowest degree of detachment is that one is never induced by the world to commit a sin, nor to neglect any act of obedience. The highest degree is that you take nothing from it unless you know that to take it is more pleasing to God than to leave it. Between these two are many degrees.

Sincere detachment has many marks. Among these is that one does not rejoice for what one possesses, nor mourn for what one does not, and that the pursuit and enjoyment of the world do not distract one from that which is better with one's Lord.

You must remove the love of Dīnārs and Dirhams from your heart until they become in your eyes as pebbles and sand. Remove the wish to be thought highly of from your heart until both people's praises and condemnations become equal to you, or whether they are attracted or repulsed by you; for the love of prominence is more harmful than that of money. Both, however, indicate desire for the world.

---

4. Bayhaqī, *Shu'ab al-Īmān,* 10068; *Al-Asmā' wa al-Ṣifāt*, 326; Al-Hākim, *Mustadrak*, 7863; Ibn Abī Shayba, *Muṣannaf*, 34314, 34315.

5. Daylamī, *Musnad al-Firdaws*, 3364; Bayhaqī, *Shu'ab al-Īmān,* 10054; Al-Shihāb, *Musnad*, 278.

6. Ibn Māja, *Sunan*, 4102; Bayhaqī, *Shu'ab al-Īmān*, 10044. The rest of the ḥadīth runs: *and do not desire what other people possess, and people will love you.*

7. Tirmidhī, *Sunan*, 2320; Ibn Māja, *Sunan*, 4110.

8. Tirmidhī, *Sunan*, 2322; Ibn Māja, *Sunan*, 4112.

9. Suyūṭī, *Al-Jāmi' al-Ṣaghīr*; Al-Muttaqī al-Hindī, *Kanz al-'Ummāl*, 6117.

The basis of the love of prominence is to love being considered great by others. Greatness is one of God's attributes, however, so that this amounts to disputing Him His Lordship.

The basis of the love of money is the love of gratifying one's desires, and this is one of the attributes of cattle. The Prophet—may blessings and peace be upon him—has said, *God the Exalted says, "Greatness is my lower garment and pride my upper garment. He who disputes Me either I shall cast into the fire of Hell."*[10] And he has said, may peace be upon him, *Two hungry wolves let loose among sheep devastate them no more than the love of prominence and money devastate one's religion.*[11]

You must always opt to take little from the world and confine yourself to your needs in matters of clothes, food, marriage, housing, or any other comfort. Beware of indulgently seeking its pleasures while claiming detachment, using arguments that are unacceptable to God, and contrived interpretations that are far removed from the truth. The way in which the Messenger of God—may God's blessings and peace be upon him—the Prophets before him, and the religious leaders after him, shunned the world's pleasures even while able to enjoy them lawfully is quite obvious to anyone who has the least knowledge.

If you are incapable of detaching yourself from the world, then admit to your desire for it, for there is no blame in this; you will only have sinned if you pursue and enjoy it in a manner forbidden by the Law. Detachment is a degree higher than this. Would that I knew—even had God the Exalted made it obligatory on us to take liberally from the world—where we will find the ability to do so at a time when it has become arduous to find even a lawful garment with which to cover oneself decently, or enough lawful food to allay one's hunger.

We are God's and to Him we shall return.[12]

10. Abū Dāwūd, *Sunan*, 4090; Ibn Māja, *Sunan*, 4175.
11. Tirmidhī, *Sunan*, 2376; Ibn Ḥibbān, *Ṣaḥīḥ*, 3228.
12. Qur'ān, 2:156.

Chapter 31

On Reliance on God

You must rely on God the Exalted, for He suffices, enriches, and is the Ally of those who do. ***And he who relies on God, God will suffice Him.***[1]

Reliance[2] [on God] is a result of *Tawḥīd* that is sincere, firmly rooted, and has prevailed in the heart. God the Exalted says, ***Lord of the East and Lord of the West, there is no god but Him, so take Him for a Patron.***[3] Notice how He begins by affirming Lordship, then the exclusive oneness of Divinity, before ordering us to rely on Him—Majestic and High is He!—thus leaving no excuse for anyone to forsake this. He commands His servants to rely on Him and encourages them to do so by saying, ***And upon God let the believers rely.***[4] And, ***So rely on God; indeed, God loves those who rely*** [on Him].[5] And the Messenger of God—may God's blessings and peace be upon him—has said, *Were you to rely on God as He rightly should be, He would provide for you as He provides for the birds which go off hungry in the morning and return full in the evening.*[6]

Know that the basis of reliance on God is the heart's knowledge that all matters are in God's hand, whether beneficial or harmful, unpleasant or pleasant, that were all creation to unite to be of benefit to someone they would benefit him only in the way which God has already written for him; and that were they to unite to harm him, they would do so only in that which God has already written against him.

1. Qur'ān, 65:3.
2. *Tawakkul* is total reliance and dependence on God, and trustfully committing oneself to Him.
3. Qur'ān, 73:9.
4. Qur'ān, 3:122.
5. Qur'ān, 3:159.
6. Tirmidhī, *Sunan*, 2344; Nasā'ī, *al-Sunan al-Kubrā*, 11805.

It is a condition for sound reliance that it does not lead you to disobey God, and that you avoid what He has forbidden and perform what He has commanded, relying in all this on Him, seeking [only] His assistance and committing yourself to Him. Using any of the world's means [secondary causes] does not invalidate your reliance as long as you rely on God and not on it. Certainly, he whose reliance is sincere, his use of worldly means will be meagre. As for totally divesting oneself of them, this is praiseworthy only for those whose approach to God is constant, whose hearts are purified from attending to anything other than Him, and who do not by so doing cause those of God's creatures whom they support to be lost. The Messenger of God has said, may God's blessings and peace be upon him and his family, *It is sufficient sin for a man to allow those he supports to be lost.*[7]

Know that saving, storing provisions, or seeking treatment for illnesses in no way compromise the essence of reliance for those who know that the One who enriches, benefits, or harms, is God alone. The Messenger of God—may God's blessings and peace be upon him—stored provisions for those in his charge to demonstrate that it was allowed; as for himself—may God's blessings and peace be upon him—he never saved anything for the morrow; and if someone else saved something for him, he forbade it as soon as it came to his knowledge. When he was asked—may peace be upon him—about the seventy thousand from his community who are to enter the Garden without prior judgment, he said, *They are those who refrain from treatment by recitation or cauterization and believe not in augury, but rely on their Lord.*[8]

The one whose reliance is sincere has three marks. The first

7. Nasā'ī, *al-Sunan al-Kubrā*, 9131; Al-Ḥākim, *Mustadrak,* 8526.

8. Bukhārī, *Ṣaḥīḥ*, 5705; Muslim, *Ṣaḥīḥ*, 218. *Ruqiā* or treatment by recitation is by placing one's hand over the patient and reciting certain verses of the Qur'ān and other formulae of *dhikr*. This is entirely legitimate so long as nothing is used that does not belong to the Qur'ān or *Sunna*; otherwise, especially if the formula is unintelligible, it will be forbidden. Cautery with fire is lawful. The Prophet did not forbid it, but discouraged people from using it, saying that he did not like his community to be treated with fire. As for augury, *taṭayyur*, the ancient Arabs used to startle the birds so that they flew off, and then they observed the direction they took. Flying off to the right side was considered a good omen, whereas flying off to the left side was considered an evil omen.

is that he neither hopes in nor fears other than God. The sign of this is that he upholds the truth in the presence of those who, like princes and rulers, usually arouse hope and fear in people. The second is that worrying about his sustenance never enters his heart, so confident is he in God's guarantee. Thus, his heart is as tranquil when in need as when his needs have been fulfilled. The third is that his heart does not become disturbed in fearful situations, in the knowledge that whatever has missed him could never have hit him, and whatever has hit him could never have missed him. An example of this was related of my master 'Abd al-Qādir al-Jīlānī, may God spread his benefit. He was once discoursing on Destiny when a great viper crawled over him, which caused his audience to panic. The viper coiled itself around the Shaykh's neck, then slipped into one of his sleeves and came out from the other, but he remained firm and unperturbed, not even interrupting his discourse. Another Shaykh who was once thrown to a lion but came to no harm was asked, "What were you thinking about when thrown to the lion?" He replied, "The legal status of lion leftovers."[9]

God is our sufficiency and He is the Best of Patrons.[10]

9. This refers to whether they are ritually clean or impure.
10. Qur'ān, 31:73.

Chapter 32

On Love and Contentment

You must love God until He becomes—Transcendent is He—dearer to you than all else, and until you come to have no other beloved. Love arises either in response to the perfection of the beloved or because good things are forthcoming from him. If you are one whose love is caused by perfection, then [know that] perfection, majesty, and beauty are exclusively God's and none shares any of them with Him. Whenever perfection or beauty are observed in created beings, they have no origin other than God's perfecting or beautifying them, for He creates and designs all beings, and should He not grace them with existence, they would remain invisible, non-existent; and but for the effusion of the lights of the beauty of His making upon them they would look ugly and sinister.[1] But if you are one whose love is motivated by what he stands to gain, then there will be no grace, favor, honor, or provision but that it is God the Exalted that will have bestowed it upon you, as upon any other created being, purely through his generosity and liberality. How beneficent has He already been to you? How many a favor has He bestowed upon you? He is your Master and Guardian, who created and guides you, to whom both your life and your death belong, who provides you with food and beverage, looks after you, nurtures, shelters, and grants you refuge. He sees very well your ugly behavior, yet conceals it; you ask Him to forgive you and He does, and He sees your righteous behavior and multiplies and manifests it. When you obey Him, it is by His providence and His aid, yet He mentions your name in the Unseen[2] and casts respect and love for you into the hearts of others. You disobey Him using His favors, yet disobedience does

---

1. Were it not for the enveloping lights of the Divine Attributes of Beauty, things would show their blemishes and look sinister, and there would remain nothing good in them at all.

2. At the Supreme Assembly (*al-Mala' al-A'lā*).

not lead Him to withhold these favors from you. How can you love other than such a Generous God and how can you disobey such a Compassionate Lord?

Know that the basis of love is knowledge and its result is contemplation [*mushāhada*]. Its lowest degree is that it should be supreme in your heart. The test of sincerity here is that you refuse invitations from persons you love to that which would incur God's anger, such as sins or the neglect of acts of obedience. Its uppermost degree is that there remains in your heart not the slightest love for other than God. This is a rare and precious thing, and to persist therein is even more so. When it does persist the human attributes fade away completely and an absorption in God obtains which leaves no room for any awareness of the existent universe and its people.

Know that love for the Messenger of God, all of God's other Prophets, angels, and virtuous servants, and everything that assists in His obedience, is but part of one's love for Him—Exalted is He. He has said, may blessings and peace be upon him and his family, *Love God for the favors He grants you, love me for the love of God, and love the People of my House for my love.*[3] And he has said, may peace be upon him, *God says, "My love is due to those who love each other for my sake, those who seek each other's company for my sake, who visit each other for my sake, and who donate to each other for my sake."*[4]

Sincere love has signs, the greatest and highest of which is perfection in one's emulation of the Messenger—may God's blessings and peace be upon him—in his speech, acts, and character. God the Exalted says, ***Say: If you love God, then follow me and God will love you.***[5] How thorough one is in emulating God's Beloved is proportionate to one's love for God; when the latter is abundant, the former will be abundant too, while if the latter is scarce, the former will be scarce too. ***And God is witness to what we say.***[6]

You must be content with God's decrees, for this contentment

3. Tirmidhī, *Sunan*, 3789; Al-Ḥākim, *Mustadrak*, 4716.
4. Aḥmad, *Musnad*, 22030; Al-Ḥākim, *Mustadrak*, 7314.
5. Qur'ān, 3:31.
6. Qur'ān, 28:28.

is among the noblest consequences of love and direct knowledge. It is the attribute of the lover to be pleased with the acts of his Beloved, whether these are sweet or bitter. He has said, may God's blessings and peace be upon him, that God says, *He who is not content with My decrees and will not patiently endure My trials, let him seek a lord other than I!*[7] And he has said, may peace be upon him, *When God loves certain people He afflicts them. He who is content is met with contentment, but he who is angry is met with anger.*[8]

Your duty, O believer, is to know and have conviction that God the Exalted is the One who causes guidance and misguidance, misery and happiness, and nearness and remoteness; He gives and withholds, abases and exalts, and brings about harm and benefit. Knowing and believing this, your duty is never to object, either outwardly or inwardly, to any of His acts. To object means to say, "Why was that?" "What was the purpose of it?" or, "Why has it not happened in this or that manner? What did so-and-so do to deserve this?" There can be none more ignorant than he who raises objections to the way God manages His kingdom, or who disputes His sovereignty, even while aware that God the Exalted is the only Creator, Sovereign, Judge, and Manager, who does what He will and decides as He wishes. ***He cannot be asked to account for what He does, while they can.***[9] On the contrary, you must believe that everything that God does cannot be done in a wiser, more equitable, better, or more perfect way.

Such is, in general terms, contentment with God's acts. To be more specific: Matters that concern you are of two kinds: [Firstly,] Those that please you, such as good health and prosperity. Resentment is inconceivable here except were you to look at those who possess more than you; your duty then is to be content with what God has allotted you because His is the right to do as He pleases in his kingdom, or better still because He has chosen what is best and most suitable for your particular circumstances. [Secondly,] that which displeases you, such as misfortunes, illnesses, and calamities. Discontent with these and panic are forbidden. It is far better

7. Ṭabarānī, *Kabīr*, 807.
8. Tirmidhī, *Sunan*, 2396; Ibn Māja, *Sunan*, 4031.
9. Qur'ān, 20:23.

to accept such things contentedly and surrender [to God's will]. If you cannot, then patiently endure for the sake of God and in expectation of reward. The Prophet has said, may God's blessings and peace be upon him and his family, *Worship God the Exalted by contentment in certainty. If you cannot, then know that in the patient endurance of that which you dislike lies much good.*[10]

Certain foolish people neglect some of their duties and commit transgressions, yet feel secure; this has nothing to do with contentment, for disobedience and neglect of one's duties are causes for God's wrath, so how can one be pleased with that which displeases Him? God the Exalted says, ***If you are ungrateful, God has no need of you, and He is not pleased with ingratitude in His servants; but if you are thankful, He approves of it for you.***[11] Such wretched people think they are pleased with their Lord, when in reality they are pleased only with themselves! Being pleased with oneself and being pleased with one's Lord are far apart and can never be joined together.

How excellent is that which Imām al-Ghazālī—may God be pleased with him—wrote to Abū al-Fatḥ al-Dimashqī—may God have mercy on him: "Contentment is to be content inwardly with God's acts, but outwardly do what pleases Him."

Should a servant wish to know how much contentment he has, then let him search for it when hardships arrive, afflictions descend, and sicknesses grow severe, for it is in such circumstances that he either will or will not find it.

One frequently hears the villains of these times, when asked why they abandon obedience and commit transgressions, reply, "This is something that God has predestined us to do; we cannot avoid it, for we are but overwhelmed slaves." This is the Fatalistic [*Jabriyya*] outlook,[12] and he who holds such an opinion is implying, although not explicitly, that there was no point in sending Messengers, or revealing Scriptures. How can someone who claims to have faith argue for himself against his Lord, when God's is the most complete argument against all His creatures?

---

10. Bayhaqī, *Shu'ab al-Īmān,* 1043, 9528; Abū Nu'aym, *Ḥilyat al-Awliyā',* 1:314.

11. Qur'ān, 39:7.

12. The Jabriyya were fatalists who held that man has no free will.

And how can a believer accept to imitate the idolaters who said, ***Had God so wished we would not have associated*** [anything with Him] ***nor would our fathers, nor would we have forbidden anything.***[13] Has he not heard God's reply to them through His Prophet, ***Say, "Have you any knowledge that you can show us? You follow nothing but conjectures; you only guess".***[14] Even the idolaters when they return to God will not be able to use such an untenable argument; on the contrary, they will say, ***Our Lord! Our evil fortune overwhelmed us and we were people astray.***[15] ***Our Lord! We have now seen and heard; send us back that we may do right; we are now convinced!***[16]

Know that supplication even with insistence does not compromise contentment; on the contrary, it is part of it. How can it not be so when prayer expresses true conviction in God's unity, is the language of servitude, and the hallmark of the realization of helplessness, neediness, humility, and poverty? Anyone who has realized these attributes has attained to knowledge and arrival, and to the utmost nearness to God. It has been related that the Messenger of God—may blessings and peace be upon him—said that *prayer is the marrow of worship,*[17] *the weapon of the believer, and the light of the heavens and earth;*[18] and that *those who fail to ask of God incur His wrath.*[19] Our Lord—Majestic is His power—says, ***To God belong the most beautiful Names; thus call on Him by them!***[20] And, ***Your Lord has said: Pray to Me and I shall answer you.***[21] That which happened to the Intimate Friend—may peace be on him—when he was cast into the flames, yet refrained from

13. Qur'ān, 6:148.
14. Qur'ān, 6:48.
15. Qur'ān, 23:106.
16. Qur'ān, 32:12.
17. Tirmidhī, *Sunan*, 3371; Ṭabarānī, *Awsaṭ*, 3196.
18. Al-Ḥākim, *Mustadrak,* 1812; Abū Ya'lā, *Musnad*, 439; Ibn Ḥajar al-'Asqalānī, *Al-Maṭālib al-'Āliya*, 3339.
19. Bukhārī, *al-Adab al-Mufrad*, 658; Tirmidhī, *Sunan*, 3373; Aḥmad, *Musnad*, 9701.
20. Qur'ān, 7:180.
21. Qur'ān, 40:60.

praying,[22] was due to the particular spiritual state he was in at the time, for otherwise, God relates many of his prayers in numerous passages of His Book; in fact, He relates more from him than from any other Prophet. Therefore, study the Book of God and extract the sciences from it, for they are all there in sum and nothing has been left out, neither the minute nor the immense, nor the manifest, nor the hidden. God the Exalted says, ***We have neglected nothing in the Book.***[23] And, ***We revealed the Book to you as an exposition of all things, a guidance, a mercy, and good news for the believers.***[24]

22. When Abraham—may peace be upon him—was cast into the fire for having destroyed the idols in the temple, Gabriel came to ask him what request to convey to God on his behalf. He replied, "His knowledge of my condition renders my prayers superfluous."

23. Qur'ān, 6:38.

24. Qur'ān, 16:90.

Conclusion

We shall quote here some Divine injunctions handed down as Holy Traditions [*Aḥādīth Qudsiyya*] and sound traditions.

The Messenger of God—may blessings and peace be upon him—repeating the words of his Lord, said, *"O my servants, I have forbidden myself injustice and made it forbidden among you; therefore, be not unjust to each other! O my servants, you are all hungry save those I feed; therefore, ask Me and I shall feed you! O my servants, you are all naked save those I clothe; therefore, ask Me and I shall clothe you! O my servants, you do wrong by night and by day, and I forgive all sins; so, ask Me and I shall forgive you! O my servants, you will never be able to benefit or harm Me. O my servants, were the hearts of the first of you and the last, the humans and the jinn, to resemble the most pious of hearts among you, it would add nothing to My kingdom. O my servants, were the hearts of the first of you and the last, the humans and jinn, to resemble the most depraved of hearts among you, it would detract nothing from My kingdom. O my servants, were the first of you and the last, the humans and the jinn, to stand on one plain and ask of Me, and were I to grant every one of them his request, it would diminish that which I possess no more than would a needle dipped into the sea. O my servants, it is but your deeds which I record for you, then give you full requital; therefore, let him who meets with good, praise God, and him who does not, blame only himself."*[1]

And he has said, may blessings and peace be upon him and his family, *God has revealed to me, "Be humble with each other, let none treat the other proudly, and let none treat the other unjustly."*[2] And he has said, may blessings and peace be upon him and his family, *I once saw my Lord in a dream*, and related the *ḥadīth* until he said, *He said, "O Muḥammad!" I said, "At your service!"*

1. Muslim, *Ṣaḥīḥ*, 2577; Bukhārī, *al-Adab al-Mufrad*, 490.
2. Muslim, *Ṣaḥīḥ*, 2865; Ibn Māja, *Sunan*, 4179.

He said, "When you pray, say, 'O God, I ask You to grant me acts of goodness, the renunciation of foul deeds, and love for the poor; and if You intend temptation for Your servants, then take me to You not having been tempted.'"[3]

And he has said, may blessings and peace be upon him and his family, *God the Exalted has said, "O son of Adam, rise to Me and I shall walk to you; walk to Me and I shall run to you.*[4] *O son of Adam, remember Me for a time at the beginning of the day and a time at its end and I shall suffice you for whatever lies in between.*[5] *O son of Adam, do not fail to pray four* rak'as *at the beginning of the day; I shall look after your interests until its end."*[6]

God revealed to Adam, may peace be upon him, "Four things contain all that is good for you and your offspring. One of these is for Me, one for you, one between you and Me, and one between you and My servants. As for the one that is Mine, it is that you worship Me and associate none with Me; as for the one that is yours, this is your deeds, for which I reward you; as for the one that is between you and Me, it is that your place is to pray and Mine to answer; and as for the one that is between you and My servants, it is that you treat them as you would like them to treat you."

It is written [in the scrolls] of Abraham, may peace be upon him, "The intelligent man should hold his tongue, know his times, and concentrate on his business. The intelligent man should divide his time into four: A time to commune with his Lord, a time to call himself to account, a time to meet with his brothers who help him gain awareness of his defects, and a time when he releases his soul to its [lawful] pleasures."

In the Torah it is said, "O Son of Adam, do not fail to stand before Me in prayer, for I am God and if your heart draws nearer to Me in the Unseen, you will behold My Light."

And in another of God's revealed Books, "O Son of Adam, I have created you for My worship, so do not play games; and I

---

3. Tirmidhī, *Sunan*, 475; Aḥmad, *Musnad*, 3484.
4. Aḥmad, *Musnad*, 15925; Ibn Ḥajar al-'Asqalānī, *al-Maṭālib al-'Āliya,* 3146.
5. Munāwī, *Al-Ithāfāt al-Saniyya bi al-Ahādīth al-Qudsiyya,* 3; Abū Nu'aym, *Ḥilyat al-Awliyā',* 8:213.
6. Tirmidhī, *Sunan*, 475; Nasā'ī, *al-Sunan al-Kubrā*, 468.

have guaranteed your sustenance, so exhaust not yourself. O Son of Adam, seek Me and you shall find Me, and when you find Me you will have found everything, but if you miss Me, you will have missed everything, for I am dearer to you than all else. O Son of Adam, I am God who says to a thing, 'Be!' and it is. Obey Me and I shall give you to say to a thing, 'Be!' and it is."

And God revealed to Moses, may peace be upon him, "O son of 'Imrān, be alert; take some brothers unto yourself, but any intimate friend or companion who does not help you to please Me is your enemy. O Moses, what have you to do with the abode of the unjust? It is no abode for you! Make it not your purpose, but separate yourself from it in your heart, for an evil place it is, save for those who do good, for whom it is an excellent place. O Moses, I shall watch the wrongdoer until I restore to those he wronged their rights. O Moses, when you see affluence approaching, say, 'A sin the punishment of which has been hastened!' But when you see poverty approaching say, 'Welcome to the inner garment of the virtuous!' O Moses, forget not My remembrance, for it is with forgetfulness that sins increase; and do not amass wealth, for it hardens the heart. O Moses, tell the wrongdoers not to remember Me, for whenever they remember Me, I shall remember them with a curse, for I have imposed upon Myself that I shall remember those who remember Me."

God revealed to one of His Prophets, upon all of whom be peace, "Tell your people not to do as My enemies do, nor wear what My enemies wear, nor eat as My enemies eat, nor ride as My enemies ride, so as not to become My enemies just as the others are My enemies."

And God revealed to David, may peace be upon him, "Find intimacy with Me, but estrangement with all else. O David, tell the Veracious among My servants to rejoice only in Me and delight only in My remembrance. O David, make My servants love Me!" David asked, "O Lord, how shall I make them love You?" And He replied, "Remind them of My favors. O David, the one who returns a runaway to Me I declare a brilliant worker. O David, when you see a seeker of Me, be his servant. O David, inquire not about Me from a scholar intoxicated by this world, for he will bar you from My path, such as highwaymen are to My servants. O David, behave as do the righteous, smile not at the depraved; keep company with My friends and contradict My enemies. O David, be a compassionate father to widows and orphans and I shall increase your provision and remit your sins. O David, lower your gaze and hold your tongue, for I do not like the corrupt, and plea abundantly for forgiveness, both for yourself and all sinners."

God revealed to one of His Prophets, upon all of whom be peace, "Remember Me when you are angry and I shall remember you when I am angry, so that I shall not pulverize you along with those I pulverize."

And God revealed to Jesus, may peace be upon him, "Tell the Children of Israel not to enter any of My houses save with pure hearts, downcast eyes, and clean bodies. Inform them that I shall never answer any of their prayers so long as they have not made reparation for injustices committed." And, "O son of Mary, counsel yourself; and then if you take heed, counsel the people; if not, then be ashamed before Me."

It has been related that God the Exalted says, "Tell those who study for other than a religious purpose, learn but not to practice, adopt the garments of piety for the sake of appearances, whose tongues are sweeter than honey, but whose hearts are more bitter than aloes,[7] is it I they have illusions about? Is it I they defy? I swear that I shall test them with a trial that shall leave the intelligent among them bewildered."[8]

God revealed to Moses, may peace be upon him, "When you see the poor, call them to account just as you do with th””e wealthy. If you do not, then bury everything that I have taught you under the dust."

And God revealed to David, may peace be upon him, "O David, tell my protégés and beloved ones to forsake their companions, for I shall comfort them with My remembrance, speak to them intimately, and remove the veil between us, that they

7. Aloe: a plant whose juice is extremely bitter.

8. Ibn 'Abd al-Barr, *Jāmi' Bayān al-'Ilm wa Faḍlih,* 1139; Qurṭubī, *Tafsīr,* 1:19. The version in Tirmidhī, *Sunan*, 2405, reads: The Prophet said, may blessings and peace be upon him, *God—Exalted is He—says, "I have created people whose tongues are sweeter than honey, but whose hearts are more bitter than aloes. By Myself do I swear, I shall test them with a trial that shall leave the intelligent among them bewildered; is it I they have illusions about? Is it I they defy?"*

may behold My Glory. Speak of Me, O David, to the people of the earth, and inform them I am the lover of he who loves Me, the companion of he who keeps Me company, the comfort of he who seeks comfort in Me, the friend of he who befriends Me; I obey he who obeys Me, and choose he who chooses Me, so come to Me to be honored, to be granted My company, and to transact with Me, for I am God, the Liberal, the Glorious. I say to a thing, 'Be!' and it is."

And God revealed to one of His Prophets, may peace be upon them, "Servant of Mine, give Me the tears of your eyes and the reverence of your heart, then call Me and I shall respond to you, for I am the Near, the Responsive. Servant of Mine, go forth to the cities and the fortresses and tell them two things on My behalf: tell them to eat nothing but lawful food and say nothing but the truth; and whenever one of them wishes to engage in an activity, let him think of its consequences; if these are good, then let him proceed, but if they are evil, then let him refrain."

And God revealed to Jesus, may peace be upon him, "Tell the Children of Israel to heed these two things from Me: tell them to be content with but little of this world for the good of their religion, just as the people of this world are content with but little of religion for the good of their world."

And God revealed to Moses, may peace be upon him, "Be as a lone bird that eats from the treetops, drinks plain water, and when night falls, seeks refuge in a cave, seeking intimacy with Me, estranged from those who disobey Me. O Moses, I have imposed upon Myself that I shall never allow the works of those who draw away from Me to be completed. I shall disappoint those whose hopes are placed in other than Me, I shall break the backs of those who lean on other than Me, I shall prolong the estrangement of those who find comfort in other than Me, and I shall turn away from those who love other than Me. O Moses, I have servants to whom I listen when they speak to Me, to whom I come when they call Me, whom I bring closer when they approach, whom I protect when they draw nearer, whose side I take when they take Mine, to whom I am true when they are true to Me, and whom I reward when they act for Me. Their affairs I shall manage, and their hearts and states I shall govern. I shall cause their hearts to find tranquility only in My remembrance, which shall be the cure of their sicknesses and the light of their hearts. They shall find solace only in Me, allow their hearts repose only with Me, and rest only when they reach Me."

And God revealed to David, may peace be upon him, "O David, give glad tidings to the sinners and warn the Veracious!" He asked, "O Lord, how shall I give glad tidings to the sinners and warn the Veracious?" He said, "Give the sinners glad tidings that no sin is too great for Me to forgive, and warn the Veracious not to admire their own works, for were I to subject them to My justice and judgment they will surely be doomed. O David, I have prescribed mercy upon Myself, and decreed forgiveness for those who request it; I forgive all sins, small and great, for they will never be too great for Me; therefore, do not doom yourself, or despair of My mercy, for My mercy envelops all things and My mercy outstrips My wrath. The treasuries of the heavens and the earth are in My hand, as is all goodness. I have created nothing out of need, but only to manifest My power and that all beholders might know the wisdom of My design and creation. O David, hear Me! Verily I say: When My servant comes to Me fearful of My chastisement, I chastise him not with My Fire. O David, hear Me! Verily I say: When My servant comes to Me, ashamed of his sins, I cause his guardians[9] to forget them, then I do not ask him about them. O David, hear Me! Verily I say: Were one of My servants persistently to commit enough sins to fill the world, and then regret it and ask for My forgiveness only once, and I know that in his heart he intends never to relapse, I cast them off him more swiftly than a bird falls down from the sky to the ground." And David said, "O my God, praise belongs to You for this! None who knows You should ever lose hope in You."

O God, give us from Your presence an immense reward, lead us along a straight path, make us of those on whom You have bestowed Your favors: ***the Prophets, the Veracious, the martyrs, and the virtuous, and the best of companions they are.***[10]

This is God's grace, and God is sufficient as Knower.[11]

9. The guardian angels who record his deeds.
10. Qur'ān, 4:60.
11. Qur'ān, 4:70.

This is the end of the treatise. Praise belongs to God firstly and lastly, inwardly and outwardly; ***He is the First and the Last, the Outward and the Inward, and He has knowledge of everything.***[12]

It is God's will. No strength is there but by God, the High, the Immense.

Praise belongs to God who guided us to this; we would never have been guided had He not guided us.[13]

It was concluded in the year 1099 of the Emigration of the Prophet, who is our leader, master, and means to our Lord, Muḥammad the Messenger of God, may the best of blessings and peace be upon him and upon his family as long as nights and days remain.

And praised be God, Lord of the Worlds!

12. Qur'ān, 57:3.
13. Qur'ān, 7:43.

GLOSSARY

Ash'arīs. Followers of the principal school of orthodox Muslim theology founded by Abu'l-Ḥasan al-Ash'arī (AD 873–935).

Baraka. Blessing; spiritual influence.

Ḥadīth Qudsī. A saying of God Himself reported by the Blessed Prophet, although not forming part of the Qur'ān.

Māturīdīs. Followers of the orthodox Muslim theological position of Abu Manṣūr al-Māturīdī (d. AD 944), today confined largely to Turkey and the Indian subcontinent.

Qibla. The direction of the Ka'ba in Mecca.

Rak'a. One unit of the regular Muslim prayer; a cycle of standing, bowing, standing again and prostrating twice.

Sādāt. Descendants of the Prophet, may God bless him and grant him peace.

Sayyid. Singular of *Sādāt*.

Siwāk. A toothbrush made from the wood of a shrub which has known antibacterial properties.

Taḥmīd. To say, 'Praise belongs to God.'

Takbīr. To say, 'God is Most Great.'

Taqwā. Awareness of God, and hence careful obedience to Him.

Tasbīḥ. To say, 'Transcendant is God!'

Wird. Any regularly repeated devotional act.

Witr. The optional prayer of an odd number of *rak'as* to be said before going to sleep at night.

Zakāt. The obligatory annual tax on wealth required by the Qur'ān.